Samuel White

**History of the American Troops, During the Late War**

Under the Command of Colonels Fenton and Campbell

Samuel White

**History of the American Troops, During the Late War**
*Under the Command of Colonels Fenton and Campbell*

ISBN/EAN: 9783743399860

Manufactured in Europe, USA, Canada, Australia, Japa

Cover: Foto ©ninafisch / pixelio.de

Manufactured and distributed by brebook publishing software (www.brebook.com)

Samuel White

**History of the American Troops, During the Late War**

# HISTORY

## OF THE

# AMERICAN TROOPS,

### DURING

# THE LATE WAR,

### UNDER THE COMMAND OF

### Colonels Fenton and Campbell,

*Giving an account of the crossing of the Lake from Erie to Long Point; also, the crossing of Niagara by the troops under Gen'ls Gaines, Brown, Scott and Porter. The taking of Fort Erie, the battle of Chippewa, the imprisonment of Col. Bull, Major Galloway, and the author (then a captain) and their treatment; together with an historical account of the Canadas.*

---

By Samuel White,
*Of Adams County, Penn.*

---

Baltimore:
PUBLISHED BY THE AUTHOR.
B. EDES, PRINTER.
1830.

Three Hundred Copies Reprinted for
GEORGE P. HUMPHREY,
Rochester, N. Y.
1896

No.

CHARLES MANN, PRINTER,
ROCHESTER, N. Y.

# PREFACE.

In presenting the following pages to the public, the author begs leave to return his warmest thanks to those of his fellow-citizens who have so liberally come forward to aid him in his undertaking. A plain man himself, he has not attempted to embellish his narrative with high-flown language, nor to impose upon the credulous, a string of fictitious adventures, but has been content with offering them a plain statement of facts, and as such he hopes it will be acceptable to the American reader.

It may be necessary to observe that in speaking of Englishmen, as the author has been forced to do, rather harshly in many places throughout this volume, he does not mean to insinuate that all of that nation are such as he has described; he has had the pleasure of knowing many, who were an honor to their country, and to whose kindness and gentlemanly conduct he feels happy in having an opportunity to testify. The contrast, also, which will necessarily be drawn between the conduct of the contending parties, resulting so eminently in favor of our own countrymen, will not be without its effect; as it will prove to those who at some future day may step forward in defence of their liberties, how much more of real and never fading glory is acquired, by the exercise of mercy and benevolence to the fallen foe, than even by the greatest valor and most distinguished generalship, unaccompanied by these attributes.

In the compilation of the work, which has been done chiefly from his notes taken at the time, he has been careful to avoid errors; some, nevertheless, owing to the disadvantages under which they were taken, may have occurred, and for these, should it prove to be so, he would bespeak indulgence.

# HISTORY
## OF THE LATE WAR.

TO repel the inroads of the British on the northern frontier, during the year 1814, the governor of the state of Pennsylvania ordered out the militia to the number of one thousand. About one half of this requisition was composed of volunteers from Cumberland county, of the eleventh division, and two companies belonging to the same division from Franklin county, and the residue was drawn from the counties of Adams and York. The detachment of the troops to which I belonged, rendezvoused at Gettysburg, on the 28th of February, 1814, and departed from that place on their march to Erie, on the tenth day of March following. On the morning of the following day, major Galloway and myself returned to Gettysburg to hold a court martial for the trial of delinquents, and after several days of arduous exertion, completed our business by the assessment of fines to the amount of upwards of *forty-thousand dollars.* Hence I returned home, news having reached me that my wife lay dangerously ill of a fever, and remained there for a short time, when upon her being pronounced convalescent, I hastened to join my companions in arms, and reached Erie, on the evening of the same day our troops arrived. We encamped on the margin of the lake, near the fort and about a mile above the town, where we remained without any occurrence of note taking place until the fourteenth of May.

About this time it was made known in camp that an expedition to Long Point was projected, and that volunteers to the number of five hundred stepped forward to assist the regular forces amounting to about four hundred men. The expedition was commanded by Col. Campbell, and all preparations having been completed on the fifteenth, we commenced crossing the lake, and landed on the Canada shore, late on the evening of the sixteenth. A company of dragoons fired on the boats that left the vessel, previous to their reaching the shore, when they put spurs to their horses and immediately rode off. We halted in a piece of woods near the lake, exposed to the rain which poured upon us all that night and next day, having no shelter except the boughs of the trees, under which we rested.

Early next morning, we crossed Buffaloe creek in a large canoe, which we were fortunate enough to find there; our troops were formed in single file, showing our whole force in front, with two small field pieces in the centre of the line, drawn by sailors and marines. In that order we marched for Dover, a very politic and ingenious mode of forming, and one well calculated to impress an enemy unacquainted with the number of our troops, with an idea of our having a very large army in the rear, this appearing only as the advance guard. A little way up the creek was situate a large store house, but it was completely emptied before we reached it, they having had information of our approach, some days before, as will be seen hereafter. We continued our march without opposition, passing over a beautiful plain, covered with luxuriant fields of wheat. When we reached Dover, we found it deserted by all but a few women, who had white clothes hanging upon broomsticks suing for peace. The only hostile demonstration on our part was, the destruction of some mills employed in manufacturing flour for the army, together with some houses occupied as stores, and those belonging to some officers, who, it had been ascertained, had been on the expedition of the burning of Buffaloe and Black Rock some time previous. Every possible respect was paid to the women and children, and the best part of the furniture in the houses which were destroyed, was even carried out by the troops previous to their being set on fire. From what information we could derive from the women, we were led to believe that they had plenty of time to have prepared for our reception, and might even, had they so chosen, prevented our landing, as they had news of our intended expedition ten days before. It appeared strange how such news should have reached them, as it was not currently known, even in our own camp, three days before we embarked, but the mystery was soon cleared up, when after we had been made prisoners, Major Galloway and I recognized in Chippewa, in company with the British officers, a gentleman whom we had formerly seen at Erie in company with our quartermaster; he must have been a spy. We took one man prisoner, whom we carried with us in our retreat. I sat with him until the last boat was ready to push off to the vessel, and then dismissed him, unhurt, and went on board. Strange as it may appear, it is not the less true, that on the very day after the British came to Dover, they burnt all the houses we had left standing, and even hung the poor old fellow whom we had had in custody.

On our return we had tempestuous weather, and were detained on the lake three days, making the continuance of our expedition five days in all. Before we had embarked on the expedition, my company had drawn rations for three days, every pound of which had been left on the shore in consequence of the badness of its quality, so that the poor fellows had nothing but bread to eat for that time; on the fourth day I prevailed upon the master of the vessel to let me have a barrel of biscuit, and one of pork for my company, which having been hoisted on deck, and the heads taken out, it was really amusing to see how soon they were emptied. In the evening we completed our landing, and arrived in safety at our camp in Erie.

Next day we learned that a general order had been given for our march to Buffaloe, and that preparations for that purpose had been commenced by Col. Fenton, when they were checked for some time by the presentation of a mutinous paper by some of the men selected for that purpose, which paper had been signed by half, if not more, of the privates in the regiment. This instrument set forth that they had determined not to march from camp, until they had received the amount of pay due them for their services, alleging as their apology, that many of them were much at a loss for shoes and other cloathing. In this situation, undecided as to what course we should pursue, we remained for several days, until at length some of the captains of companies, attached to the regiment, conceiving that something more decisive ought to be attempted to compel the mutinous portion of the regiment to return to their duty, addressed a communication to the Colonel, setting forth that they held themselves and companies in readiness to march at a minute's warning. After this a new impulse was given to preparations, and the order of march was fixed for the day following.

But the spirit of mutiny was still alive, and secret resolutions were formed amongst the disaffected, to obey no orders until the terms for which they held out were complied with, and on the following day when according to the orders, at the third roll of the drum the tents should have fallen, a number remained standing, and those who were willing to obey orders, had to be detached for the purpose of pulling them down, which however, they were permitted to do, unmolested.

While the wagons were lading, I had occasion to proceed to the centre of the regiment, having some business to transact with one of the field officers, and upon my return was waited on by Lieutenant Gardner, who informed me that during my absence a private from Capt. Roberts' company, had been amongst my men encouraging them to stand firm to their agreement, and oppose the march, and had moreover instructed them that the others had agreed to commence forming a line, which he urged them to imitate. This man was supposed to be their ringleader, and to have been appointed their commander. As the first step towards the suppression of this mutiny, I determined upon his arrest, hoping that prompt and decisive conduct in this instance would not be without its effect, in deterring the others from a continuance in the course which they adopted. Accordingly having ascertained from the Lieutenant that he could recognise him, I forthwith proceeded to the place where Roberts' company were stationed, and upon his being pointed out, immediately arrested him, and sent him to the block house, used as a guard house, and under the command of Major Marlin, a regular officer. Returning to my company I found that several of my men had already fallen into line, and that others were quickly following their example. To my demand of why they formed or by whose orders, I was unable to obtain an answer, and ordered them to disperse under pain of immediate arrest, and await the regular orders, which after some little hesitation, I succeeded in accomplishing.

The order was now passed to form line, and prepare to march ; the peaceable portion of the men immediately fell into rank, leaving a number strolling about, as if undecided what course to pursue. While in the act of walking round, enquiring from each individual his reasons for not obeying orders, and just as I had placed under arrest a couple who were conspicuous as spokesmen, and who had positively and most impertinently refused to comply, I was called to by one of my men, who bid me take care, as one of those in my rear was loading his gun to shoot me. I instantly wheeled round, sprang upon him, wrested the gun from him, and despatched him also to the guard house. The most determined being now removed, and the others left to their own discretion, aided no doubt, in the decision by Major Marlin, who, having loaded the gun in the block house with grape and cannister, commenced running them out of the port holes directed towards us ; the line was promptly formed, the order of march given, and the regiment moved off in perfect order. Another circumstance no doubt, contributed largely in restoring order, viz.: when Captain Roberts was informed that I had placed one of his men under arrest, he immediately sent to Major Marlin, requesting his liberation. Major M. applied to me to know the nature of the offence, for which the prisoner had been committed. Upon my informing him, that he had been sent there for mutinous conduct, his reply was— " I will not release him even at the command of your Colonel, until he has first undergone trial for his offence."

This answer was soon rumored about, and perceiving that the business was assuming rather too serious an appearance, the disaffected were somewhat panic struck, and there is every reason to believe that it afforded another and a strong inducement, for their return to duty.

We pursued our march that day over a road running parallel with the lake, and in some places, immediately along the beach for a considerable distance, and found it very fatiguing, owing to the deepness of the sand. The country along the lake shore was generally hilly, and seemed to be well supplied with game. We crossed two or three streams of water on our march, the principal of which was Cattaraugus creek, which we were compelled to cross in a boat. On the opposite side was situated a small village with two or three public houses. Here the soil appeared to be very good, as was the case as far as we could perceive, whenever the road diverged from the margin of the lake. Near the village just mentioned was an Indian settlement, composed of the tribe called the Cattaraugus Indians. After our encampment for the night, which we did upon the bank of the creek, we were visited by a number of them and their squaws, who appeared very much pleased to see us, more particularly as they understood we were going to fight the *British*. There seemed to be a great scarcity of men in that portion of New-York state, many, I presume, had been killed by the enemy, at the time of the burning of Buffaloe and Black Rock, as they had been called out *en masse*, previous to that transaction.

In many places along the road, the houses were literally crammed with ladies, collected there to see us as we passed through the county, and here I would strongly recommend all who may be in want of handsome wives to visit the borders of lake Erie, for I have never seen, before or since, in any part of the county, more beautiful and elegant looking ladies.

We at length reached Buffaloe without any disaster, except the loss of a few men by desertion, if indeed such an occurrence may justly be so termed, and found there quite a respectable body of regulars, consisting of two brigades. We encamped and remained there drilling our troops until the second of July, when general orders were issued for embarkation at daylight of the following morning. So unexpected was this order, and so completely had Gen. Brown concealed his intentions, that his officers, not at all suspecting the meditated movement, had actually made preparations for the celebration in camp of the Fourth of July, and had engaged his company at dinner. The immediate consequences, as will be seen, of such good policy on the part of the General, was the capture by surprise of Fort Erie on the third, without bloodshed. To return to our narrative; the army consisting of two brigades, were landed on the opposite shore without the least opposition. The first brigade under the command of Gen. Scott, and the artillery corps commanded by Major Hurdman, landed nearly a mile below whilst Gen. Ripley with the second brigade made the shore about the same distance above. Thus the fort was soon completely invested. A battery of long eighteens was immediately planted in a position which commanded it, and a flag dispatched, demanding a surrender, and granting two hours for that purpose, at the expiration of which time, the garrison consisting of 137 men, including officers, marched out and surrendered themselves prisoners of war. Several pieces of ordnance and some military stores were found in the fort.

Having reduced Fort Erie, the General immediately proclaimed martial law. His proclamation set forth, that persons demeaning themselves peaceably, and attending to their private business should meet with no interruption, whilst those found in arms should be treated as enemies. Private property, he pledged himself, should be held inviolate, but public property should be seized wherever found, and sold by the commanding General. Plundering was strictly prohibited—from the regular army the Major General had no fears, and those honorable men who had pressed forward to the standard of their country, to avenge her wrongs and gain a name in arms, would scorn to be guilty of any act, which might, in even so remote a manner reflect disgrace upon their national character.

The necessary arrangements for the preservation and garrisoning the Fort Erie, being concluded, Gen. Brown determined to march forward on the following day, and attack the enemy who lay entrenched in his works upon the plains of Chippewa. To this resolution, considered of a desperate and dangerous character, the General was doubtless urged by the necessity which he felt existed, to redeem the reputation which had been lost by the events of former campaigns—dangers and remonstrances were therefore entirely disregarded. The ardor and desire for battle was even increased by the knowledge that the glory of the victory would be so much the more brilliant, besides having formed his resolutions and plans, he was determined upon attempting their execution.

Before day-break on the morning of the fifth, it was ascertained, that the Colonel to whom orders had been sent by Gen. Porter to supply the troops with three days' provisions, had neglected that necessary precaution; the consequence was, that a boat had to be despatched to Buffaloe with an order for provisions, which however, did not reach us until about two o'clock in the day, when we were supplied with a couple of biscuits each, being the first which a majority of us had eaten that day. At four o'clock we came in view of the encampment of our regular troops, and halted. We had not been many minutes at rest before a requisition was made for volunteers to turn out and drive off the hostile Indians who had been firing on our pickets. Fatigued as we were, having traveled that day about eighteen miles without rations, it is not to be wondered at, that not much alacrity was showed by the men to become of the party. Lieut. Gilleland, Ensign Graff, the surgeon of the volunteers, and myself, laid aside our swords, and borrowing rifles, volunteered as privates; about three hundred of the volunteers of our own regiment also came forward, and these were strengthened by several hundred Indians, the whole under the command of Gen. Porter, Col. Bull and Major Galloway. I had eaten nothing except one biscuit from the time I had my dinner the day before at Buffaloe, and had even given away the balance of my store, expecting to get a good supper that evening; but I was doomed to be mistaken.

Orders were issued that every white man who went out under Gen. Porter should leave his hat, and go uncovered. The Indians tied up their heads with pieces of white muslin, and it was really diverting to see them making their preparations for battle, After having tied up their heads, which process must have consumed at least fifty yards of fine muslin, they painted their faces, making red streaks above their eyes and foreheads—they then went to old logs and burnt stumps, and spitting upon their hands rubbed them upon the burnt part, until they were perfectly black, when they drew their fingers down their cheeks leaving large black streaks—after this preparation they were ready for action or march. We proceeded in single file through a lane to our left, and in the course of half an hour came in contact with the enemy, who were posted in the woods on our right, and completely concealed from our observation. Immediately upon our entering a long narrow path, they opened upon us with a pretty brisk fire—we faced to the right and pressing forward put them to rout. They continued their flight and we pursued them, keeping up a smart fire, which, from the manner of the position, did considerable damage, until they drew us into rather a perilous situation. The whole British army had crossed the bridge at Chippewa, and drawn up their forces under cover of a piece of woods, near the Niagara river, and running parallel with the Chippewa creek, directly across the creek, where the British batteries commanded the same position. Driving the Indians rapidly through the woods, we at length came in full contact with the British regular line, which in conjunction with the batteries, opened a most tremendous fire. From the clouds of dust and heavy firing, General Brown concluded that the entire force of the British was in motion, and gave orders to General Scott to advance with his brigade and Towson's artillery, and meet the enemy on the plain in front of the American camp. In a few minutes Scott was in close action with a far superior force of regulars. Major Jessup commanding the battallion on the left flank, finding himself pressed both in front and rear, and his men falling fast, ordered his battallion to support arms and advance, which bold order in the midst of the enemy's hottest fire, was obeyed with a promptness which did them honour. Having advanced within twenty paces of the enemy's line, they were ordered to level and fire, causing such havoc in the enemy's line as forced them to retreat. About this time, also one of our hot shot fell into the enemy's magazine and blew it up—this occurrence silenced their artillery—the whole British force fell back, and being closely pressed by the American troops, retreated in confusion to their entrenchment, about a quarter of a mile distant. Gen. Brown immediately ordered the ordinance to be brought up with the intention of forcing the works, but upon more mature reflection, and by the advice of his officers, he was induced to order the forces back to camp. In this engagement, which resulted so disastrously to the British, a considerable portion of the army, though burning for the conflict, had not an opportunity of coming into action. The conquerors of the veterans of France, were, in fact, defeated by a detachment from the American army. The only troops engaged on the part of Gen. Brown, were Scott's brigade, and the Pennsylvania volunteers, commanded by Porter—the conduct of these men was heroic in the extreme; wherever they directed their fire, or pointed their bayonets, the boasted "conquerors of the peninsula" fell or fled; the volunteers, in particular manifested all the coolness and bravery of regular troops. Such was the punishment they received in this engagement, that, although battle was offered them again on their own terms, they shrunk from its acceptance.

The loss of the enemy was nearly six hundred killed, as was ascertained some time afterwards, although they were never willing to acknowledge it so great; they removed, however, off the field, nearly five hundred wounded men before their retreat, and the loss in the woods of the Canadian militia, by our scouting party, was upwards of eighty killed. It was not known how many Indians fell, but their loss must have been very great. When our scouting party returned, there were but twenty men missing, five of that number were prisoners, four whites and one Indian.

I was nearly on the extreme right of our line, which was very much extended in our progress through the woods, in consequence of broken trees, thickets, &c., and did not immediately hear the order for retreat, consequently, was slow in following the example of several of those in my rear, whom I perceived retreating; and it was not until my left had been entirely deserted, and those on my right were rapidly falling away, that I made my way with some others to a field which lay on our right. On coming to the fence, we perceived the British light horse advancing along the opposite side of the field in full speed; we immediately perceived that our chance of escape in that direction was small, as we would be taken long before we should have crossed. We then shifted our course, keeping under cover of the wood, until we had reached the end of the field, where we fell in with Col. Bull and Major Galloway, who had been more on the left. We were now on the very ground, over which, a short time before, we had driven the Canadians and Indians, and concluded ourselves in perfect safety; but we had not proceeded more than a few rods, when we suddenly found ourselves surrounded by Indians who had been lying in ambush—unable to surround us all, they had permitted a number of friendly Indians, and several of our volunteers to pass by unmolested, that they might the better secure us. After having disposed of us, a small party of them pursued those whom they had suffered to pass, several of whom, however, made good their retreat.

Having disarmed us, the first enquiry was for money. A large Indian came up to me, calling out "money, money."—I insisted that I had none. He then seized my coat, which he took off me, another claimed my vest, another my neck-cloth, and so on, until they had stripped me of every article of cloathing, except my shirt and pantaloons. It was fortunate for me my shirt was not ruffled, or they would have taken even that; they took from me a ruffled sham, which I wore over my shirt; a fellow had placed his hand upon my watch chain, with a view of drawing it from my pocket, but meeting with some little difficulty in consequence of my pocket being damp from perspiration, he deliberately drew his knife, when not wishing to give the gentleman the trouble of operating, I drew it out and handed it to him.

At the time these savages were stripping me, others were as busily engaged in dealing out in like manner to Col. Bull and Major Galloway—they took the Major's boots, compelling him to walk bare-footed. We proceeded on our march, well guarded, and had not gone more than about half a mile, when an Indian in the rear suddenly whooped loudly, raised his rifle, and shot Col. Bull through the body; the ball entered at the left shoulder, and passed out through the right breast. After he had been shot, he raised himself upon his elbow, and reached out his hand to Major Galloway asking him for assistance. At this moment the fellow who had fired came up, sunk his tomahawk in his head, scalped him, and left his body where he fell; thus perished as gallant, and noble hearted a fellow, as ever drew the sword in defence of his country. I was then unable to account for an act so contrary to all laws of warfare, and expected every moment that we should have shared the fate of our unfortunate friend.

I was afterwards informed by a Canadian gentleman, with whom I had formed an acquaintance while at Ives' Creek, that the murder was committed in compliance with the order of Gen. Rial, who had given the Indians positive instructions not to spare any who wore the uniform of militia officers, he at the same time gave them a minute description of the dress of the militia and regular officers, the latter of whom, should any be captured, they were ordered to bring into camp in safety. Now if Gen. Rial gave such orders, and that he did, I have good reason to believe, how very degrading to a civilized people is such conduct, how barbarous, worse, infinitely worse than the cruelty of the untutored savage? Startled by the whoop, I had just looked over my shoulder, and was struck motionless, petrified, by the sight; but my conductors did not allow me much time for contemplation, but hurried me forward at even a more rapid rate.

That we were not murdered as we expected, was owing to our being dressed in the uniform of the regular troops, with which we had provided ourselves before our departure from Gettysburg—the unfortunate Colonel was dressed in the old uniform of the Pennsylvania militia, and met his disastrous fate in consequence of a trifling inattention—so frail and slender are the threads upon which human life and human prosperity are dependent. Col. Bull was a man of sober and exemplary habits, and highly esteemed by the soldiery—he was a pious man, and his mind had a strong religious cast. Whilst at Erie, the most part of his Sabbaths were spent in the hospitals, in reading, conversing upon, and explaining the scriptures to the sick and disabled—but to return to our narrative, the savages who conducted me, were now hurrying me forward at a trot. Several times during our flight,

Major Galloway asked them whether they intended to kill him and Captain White, their answer was, they would not, but it will readily be believed, that after the dreadful sight we had just witnessed, we did not place much confidence in their assertions. Having cleared the woods, we now reached a green field, in running through which, the Indian who held me by the arm, and I, both trying for the furrow, jostled each other, and he fell, but still holding his grip, was instantly on his feet again. At that moment the hope of liberty flashed strongly over my mind, and had he been the only Indian with me, I would most certainly have dispatched him, or at least made the attempt; but a moment's reflection served to convince me that any effort of that kind would be attended only with instant death, and under these considerations of the case, I concluded that my safest plan was to desist from so hazardous an exploit. Coming out of the grain field, near Chippewa Creek, we were in sight of the bridge, over which the last of the British army then in view, had just crossed, the American cannon were playing briskly on the rear; the Indians who led me, for we had entirely outrun those who conducted Galloway, became alarmed, dreading that the whole army would have passed, and the bridge be destroyed, before they should be able to reach it, and accordingly turned and ran up the creek for some distance, the Indians who left Galloway, now hallooed to them, when they wheeled, and came in view of the rear guard of the British army, at the moment they were on the point of crossing the bridge. I was dreadfully fatigued, and to hurry me on, a fellow was placed behind me, who every minute or so, fixed his hands upon my shoulders, pushing me forward with a violence that well nigh threw me on my face. Faint and exhausted, I still hurried forward, exerting all my nerve, fearing that if I failed or fell, the tomahawk, the sound of which still ran in my ears, would soon give me my quietus; I had hopes too, that the moment of my deliverance from these wretches was not far distant, as I fully expected to be taken ont of their hands as soon as we should have reached the British army. In this manner we gained the bridge just as the last of the rear guard had got on it, the American round shot still rolling after us; one of them fell within a yard of me as I pressed forward, making the clay fly all over us, and then bounded into the creek; having completed our crossing, the bridge was cut down.

What was my astonishment and indignation, when having come in company with those from whom I expected relief to find them even worse than the savages, and that instead of respiting us, they encouraged them to run us still further, crying out who have you got there, a damned Yankee?—Yes—well damn him, run him well, he's not half run yet; although I then thought it impossible for me to proceed twenty rods further without dropping down dead. Thus situated, my mouth stretched wide open panting for breath, I was compelled to run between one and two miles further, to the Indian encampment, still shoved forward as before, whenever I slackened my pace; my persecutors encouraged and cheered on by the brutal and unfeeling soldiery, who seemed to look upon the affair as mere amusement.

We were sent to the rear of the camp, and here, for the first time, I was permitted to sit down; in fact I was so weakened by previous fatigue, as to be unable to stand without support. Having recruited as much breath as enabled me to speak, I asked for a drink of water; they not understanding the language, I made a sign for what I wanted, when I was led between two to a pond, where I was permitted to drink—those only who have felt the same pressing necessity, can form any idea of the luxury of that draught. They then led me back, and I again resumed my seat on the ground. A few minutes afterwards I was surrounded by thirty or forty of these savages, all armed, they brought down their guns at an order and commenced to talk—here I sat for some time perfectly silent, but at length looking up at the fellow who had had me in custody, I asked him if they were going to kill me? He snatched up his rifle and raising it in both hands brought it down with violence—he checked the fall, however, before it reached my head, and set it down as before, and casting at me a scowl of rage and hatred, resumed his place in the circle, from which the momentary act alluded to had moved him. It may be well presumed that I had no very great anxiety to ask more questions.

Two or three Canadian officers now came up, one of whom appeared perfectly versed in the language; after some conversation between him and the Indians, they opened the ring and admitted him to me; he asked a number of questions, where I was from? whether I was an officer or private? and whether I knew if there were any other officers made prisoners, and if so whether I would not like to be with them? I informed him that Major Galloway was a prisoner, in the British camp, and that I should be much pleased to have his company—he commenced another talk with the Indians, and in a few minutes they began to disperse; after the crowd had pretty well cleared away, two of them came to me and taking me by the arms, one at each side, walked me back to the British camp, where we found Major Galloway still sitting on the ground, with his Indian guard beside him. We proceeded together and were in a few minutes brought into the presence of General Rial, who immediately commenced interrogating us, asking a number of questions, the truth of which I was determined he should not know from me. One of his questions as to what number of troops we had, was addressed to Major Galloway, who seeming to hesitate, I answered for him, saying that we had something like five thousand; he replied that is not true sir, you know it is not, you have more than double that number. Had I then been acquainted with my privileges as a prisoner of war, I should not have made him an answer, as it was I excused myself, by telling him that I had computed them at that number from having seen them on parade, and had never heard from any official source, what was the actual number of men in service. He then enquired our grade, and whether we were in the regular service, or in the militia, upon our replying that we belonged to the Pennsylvania volunteers—he exclaimed what business had you to cross the frontier? We crossed, sir, in obedience to orders. Who could give such orders, sir, I thought no militiaman or volunteer could be ordered out of the United States? They can, sir, in case of insurrection or invasion. Well, sir, have you an insurrection among you? No, thank heaven, and I hope we never shall, but, sir, we have invasion. How is that, sir? where? I replied, have you not Fort Niagara in your possession? Then, sir, said he, why did you not go there? I answered, we were not ordered there. When I complained that we had been badly treated, having had our clothes stripped off us, that we had been robbed of money to the amount of about one thousand dollars, and that all we requested was to have our clothes returned as we were not accustomed to going naked, he give us to understand that all the Indians got was legitimate spoil and could not be returned—he then called two sergeants, and gave one of them orders to take that fellow, meaning me, and keep him safe 'till to-morrow morning, when I shall demand him at your hand—to the other he gave similar directions concerning Galloway, and turning upon his heel with a smile, joined his officers who were seated outside of the door on benches round a table covered with glasses. I forgot to state, that when I had informed him of the murder of Col. Bull, and that he had been scalped by the Indians, his reply was—I do not believe he has been scalped, assigning at the same time as his reason for not so believing, that at that time they gave nothing for scalps.

We were now carried off by the sergeants and separated—we were compelled to be behind the breastworks, on the bare ground, without tent or covering of any kind. I suffered severely from the cold, in consequence of having been overheated during the day, and then stripped of my cloathing. In the night I took a chill, and shook as if I had had the ague; I am confident I should have perished but for the humanity of the sergeant, who had charge of me, in lending me his old watch coat, and a handkerchief to tie round my head; he also gave me a dram from his canteen—he, poor fellow, had been a prisoner amongst the Americans, and candidly acknowledged, that he had been well treated. In the morning he applied for rations for Galloway and myself, and returned without having been able to obtain any—this was continued for three days in succession, during which time we sustained life merely through the charity of our friendly guard. On the first morning after the battle, having heard that a flag of truce was about to be sent to the American camp, asking the privilege of burying their dead, I enquired whether a letter would be carried for me, and was told it would, but that it must be sent open. Being kindly furnished by the sergeant with pen and paper, I wrote a note merely stating that we were prisoners, requesting that our clothes, and if possible, a little money might be sent to us, as we were suffering severely from want of them. Fearful that the letter might not be sent, if it contained any thing offensive, I forebore to mention either the death of Col. Bull, or our own treatment. On the return of the flag, I enquired if my letter had been delivered and what answer; the letter had been delivered but they had no answer whatever. I was also informed, that to their request to be allowed to bury the dead, Gen. Brown replied that he was able to bury all the men he could kill.

On the afternoon of the third day I saw one of the British light horse coming down the Chippewa at full speed; he kept his horse under whip and spur, until he arrived at the officers' quarters, and in a few minutes the camp was all bustle. The artillery horses were speedily driven under the whip up the Chippewa at a round pace; the baggage wagons were loading in all quarters, and in a few minutes the artillery opened a brisk fire; they had not fired many rounds before I heard our long eighteens speaking in return. I felt rejoiced at the sound, believing that they must be beaten should a general engagement ensue, and that in the interim I might have a fair chance of escape. However during the cannonade the British army was formed in line and led into the field, Major Galloway, two of our volunteers, one Indian, myself and three or four Canadians who were in confinement, on suspicion of being friendly to the American cause, were led into the field under a strong guard and halted to await the fate of the day. The British artillery was soon silenced, the captain as I afterwards understood had been killed, several others severely wounded, and one of their cannon dismounted, by having the carriage wheels blown away. They now retired nearly as fast as they advanced, and by this time the baggage wagons being loaded, were moved forward on the road to Fort George, and orders being giving to retreat, they set off at full trot, and some in a gallop, not delaying to pick up the camp kettles, which were dropping along the road, one here, one there, shaken from the wagons by the unusually rapid motion; the army moved off at quick step, and we were marched in the rear, still surrounded by our guard. In this manner we proceeded until we came to Lundy's Lane, where they were met by a reinforcement from Queenstown heighths; they called a halt for a few minutes, during which the officers held a council, at the close of which the reinforcement was wheeled round and the retreat continued. When we reached Queenstown heighths we were halted before a house, at which were a number of British officers; I was then brought in front, and viewed by some of them, who not being able to discover in me an old acquaintance, I was remanded to my former station. This examination was owing to information having been lodged by a fellow who had seen me the day after I had been made prisoner, that I had belonged to a certain British regiment, the name of which I do not remember; that I had deserted and gone over to the United States, and had received my commission as a reward; he had sworn most blasphemously to the truth of his assertions, and concluded with "d——n you, I will have you hung"; I, however, heard no more of the business; we were then marched forward on the road to Fort George, and after some time diverged to the right and proceeded nearly two miles to a large brick house, where we were confined up stairs, having one guard at the room door, one at the head of the stairs and one at the outer door; part of the army also had encamped round the house, around them was stationed a camp guard, and outside of all was stationed a picket guard, all to take care of four American prisoners, and one Indian. The rest of the troops continued their march to Fort George. Had any of us made our escape at that time, it would have been highly injurious to them, as their forces were much weakened by previous losses. I know that they had two vessels so completely crammed with wounded men, that the other prisoners and myself were obliged to remain on deck the whole time of the passage from Fort George to York, where we were landed.

The wounded officers were carried to town in blankets by four men one at each corner.

And here I should be committing an act of ingratitude, did I not notice the kind manner in which we were treated by a gentleman, named Carr, a doctor, who overtook us on our march from Chippewa to Fort George, and a short distance from the former place. In conversation with me he stated that he had two sons, Captains in the British army, that one of them had been for some time a prisoner amongst the Americans, and that he had been well treated, that the other had been taken at the battle of Chippewa, and that this was the first time he had had it in his power to evince his gratitude to any of the American Officers; he at the same time requested me to receive a twenty dollar bill, and divide it with my companion Major Galloway; in our circumstances it was a very acceptable present; we were still almost naked, and it was evening of the third day since the battle of Chippewa, and we had not as yet been supplied with rations, and were obliged to march part of the afternoon nearly eleven miles. He returned in a few minutes afterwards with a five dollar bill, which he told us he had collected from some of the officers, and which he entreated me to divide among the other prisoners, or apply to their use by buying necessaries for them, which was accordingly done. We were several days at Fort George before the vessels were ready to sail for York. Late in the afternoon of the fourth day after we had been made prisoners, we were furnished with rations—we ate our beef as it came out of the pickle, as we could not think of waiting to cook it.

While we remained there, an officer, who from his dress, appeared to belong to the dragoons, called to see the Major and myself, and in course of conversation, asked us if we had any tea or sugar, or any liquors; he continued to converse some time in a very agreeable manner, and then took his leave. A short time after he had gone, we had a visit from his servant, who brought us a paper of tea, some sugar, and a bottle of rum. All the time we drew rations we were never allowed any liquor, and got none except the one bottle thus made a present of. This treatment was very different from what they, when made prisoners by us, experienced—if any part of the rations were scarce, our own men have stinted themselves in order that the prisoners might be supplied—this I know to be a fact, as the men belonging to my own company have gone without their liquor, that prisoners might be better accommodated. The evening after Galloway and I were made prisoners, and were almost perishing with cold and hunger, with the damp ground alone for our bed, and the canopy of heaven for our covering, the British officers made prisoners by our troops, were feasted with the best the camp could afford. The officers of my own company had killed a fat calf, in order to have something nice to give them for supper; as they were strangers, they wished to entertain them well, and would have been happy to have had all the officers in the British army in the same situation, were it only to afford them a more ample field for the exercise of their generosity—but to return. We were marched into York, and halted for about half an hour at a tavern; here we applied to the landlady, to know if she could provide us change of linen; we had been then upwards of two weeks without change. She furnished us with two old shirts more than half worn for which, however, we had to pay her the *moderate* price of eight dollars.

We were then asked if we would accept of paroles to go to Montreal, stating at the same time that if we did, we should be furnished with money and horses, and if we did not, we would be sent on board a boat under guard. We concluded that it would be better for us to accept the terms offered, than to be dragged under guard through the country; however, we did not profit much by our compliance, for an hour had scarcely passed, after we had signed the parole, when we were ordered on board a Durham boat, to be sent under guard to Kingston. The British officers on board, when night came on, went ashore, and always took Galloway and myself with them, we lodged in a house convenient to the vessel; the others prisoners were suffered to remain on board, under guard.

We now found that we had acted unadvisedly in accepting of paroles, as we found several friends here who were anxious to secrete us until the British were gone, and then they promised us a safe landing on the American shore. These friendly and tempting offers, our inconsiderateness in signing paroles, completely prevented our accepting. Hence we were taken to the mouth of Ives' creek, about eighteen miles below York, where we put up for the night. For several days past, I had been very unwell, owing to fatigue and exposure to the damp night air, having lain out a few nights before. I was taken with a violent pain in my head, which lasted for nearly two hours, I then obtained a little rest, lay down in the boat, and fell asleep when the crew went ashore; the officers also went off, leaving me under care of the guard. Having slept for some time, I awoke almost perished, and calling to the guard, who had lit a fire on shore, they threw me a plank, by means of which, I got out dry. Before I had well warmed myself, I was taken intolerably sick, so much so indeed, that I could not stand up—they furnished me with a blanket, and I lay down on the beach by the fire. When I woke in the morning, I was wet to the skin, the blanket having absorbed all the moisture from the sand. All that day I remained very ill, and upon reaching Mr. Ives', was compelled to go to bed. Next morning, notwithstanding my sickness, I was marched on board, but the wind being dead ahead, and blowing fresh, we could not sail, and consequently returned to the house. On the following day, my fever had gained so much as to preclude all possibility of my being removed, in fact, I was completely deranged. In this state they made me sign a parole, and an article binding myself to be accountable for John Hughes, should he make his escape—this man was a private in my own company and had been made prisoner with me; they had determined to leave him to wait on me. So unconscious was I, at the time I signed the paper, that I knew nothing of the circumstance, until after my recovery, when I was informed of the circumstance by Major Galloway. I remained in a very bad state for eight or ten days, entirely given up by the medical gentleman who had been appointed by government to attend me; he had informed the family that they must expect my death, and so firmly were they convinced of it, that they actually prepared a shroud for me, and Mr. Ives was looking out a snug corner in one of his fields, in which to deposit me.

Matters were in this train, when chance, or my better fortune brought an old Yankee Doctor, as they called him, and who was Mr. Ives' family physician, on a visit to the house—having seen me, and examined the medicine which was administering to me, he pronounced my case as desperate, but at the same time expressed an opinion that something might yet be done for me—he accordingly commenced operations by having all the remaining medicines prescribed by my former physician, thrown out, and ordered me a treatment directly the reverse; whether it was owing to this change of practice, or that the crisis of the disease had arrived, I am not sufficiently versed in medicine to pass opinion upon, but by twelve o'clock that night, I had changed so much for the better, as to have recovered my reason, and from that time forward my progress to perfect health was slow indeed, but sure. To the kindness of a gentleman, a doctor, who resided in the neighbourhood, and who, during the first stages of my illness, had called once or twice to see me, and prescribed for me until such time as the government doctor commenced attendance, and to another, also a neighbour, and a namesake, a Mr. White, I take this opportunity of paying the tribute of my best and warmest thanks, (the poor man's only guerdon) for their liberality in supplying me with clothing, acts as grateful to me, as they were honorable to them. When I had recovered sufficiently well to see company, I had many visitors from several miles distance, who always came after dark, and returned the same night; they were very anxious to know what was the intention of the United States in sending troops into Canada, and if they had determined upon taking it—if such, they said, was our intention, a powerful party in Canada might be raised to assist in the undertaking, providing the United States government would give assurance of the fact; but that so much had they been deceived by Gen. Hull, that nothing could or would be done until such time as they had something satisfactory to rely upon. There were an immense number of men at that time disaffected with government, and had the United States deemed it expedient, or possessed the means of sending a large army into *Canada*, with the avowed purpose of freeing them from British dominion, numbers would have flocked to our standard, and they might with reason have trembled for their possessions—but to return.

About this time, a great sensation was caused by the landing, during the night, of a boat, about two miles below, with three or four well armed men on board, who, stationing themselves on the mail road, shot the horse of the mail rider, and carried off the mail, no doubt with a view to obtain news of the army, they also made prisoners, a colonel of militia, and his son, who was also an officer in the militia. They took them with the mail rider, to the beach of the lake, where having stove a parcel of flour lying there, they threw it into the water—they then compelled the prisoners to gather wood, and cook their victuals for them; after which they were paroled, and the depredators went off unmolested.

The next day I had a visit from Major Rogers, who seemed alarmed for my safety, and said that he had expected some of my friends had been to see me, and had carried me off. I replied that I believed there was not much danger of my escape, and that I should look well into whose hands I surrendered myself a prisoner again, as I had been one once too often already. He said he would not trust me, and that as soon as my health was sufficiently established to allow of my removal, he would have me carried into the country, so as to be at a distance from the lake.

A few days afterwards he called again, in company with a physician, who having examined me, declared me unfit for removal—the visit was continued from time to time, until the doctor at last pronounced me sufficiently strong for removal. During my residence with Mr. Ives, himself and family treated me with the greatest hospitality—had I been a relative, they could not have exerted themselves more for my benefit—they have my highest esteem, and highly deserved recompense, which, had I the power, I would gladly make. I was now removed some miles back into the country, where I remained for ten or twelve days, and was then put on board a boat under the care of Lieutenant Norris, a Canadian militia officer, who had orders from Major Rogers to take me to Kingston. Rogers was himself a militia officer, a devoted monarchist, and in consequence of his zeal, was then, though stationed at home under full pay from his government, being kept there to have an eye to the inhabitants, and prevent them from making their escape to the United States. In many places along Lake Ontario, the inhabitants had deserted their homes and farms, and made their way good to the United States; several were compelled to fly to save their lives, as a single word said against the government, at that time, was sufficient to hang them. Those who were brought prisoners from Fort George to York, at the time we were brought on there, on suspicion of being friendly to the American cause, were, as I afterwards understood, hanged, and some even without judge, jury, or the common formalities of a trial.

Arrived at Kingston, I was handed over to the commanding officer of that post, together with a letter of recommendation from Major Rogers. As soon as he had read the letter, he ordered me into close confinement. This I expected, from having a knowledge of the contents of the letter, given me by an officer under promise of secrecy; he at the same time promised me his influence in obtaining my release from confinement. The letter went on to state, "that I was not a commissioned officer of the United States, but had headed a party of depredators, who had come into Canada for the sole purpose of plundering the inhabitants, and therefore to show me no favors." What could have been Major Rogers' inducement to pen such a notoriously manifest falsehood, I cannot divine, unless for the mere gratification of his vile disposition, and the rancorous hatred he bore to every one who professed republican principles; at home he bore the name of a tyrant and was generally despised.

I will relate a circumstance which will serve more fully to explain his character.—While recovering, and before I had been able to leave my room, he came to see me, and after strutting about for a considerable time, gave me to understand that the United States would shortly be compelled to surrender, as the British troops had taken their Capitol, Washington. Mr. Ives fearing the effect such information might have upon me in my then reduced state, endeavored to change the conversation by telling the Major how very bad I had been; he interrupted him with the remark,—" Oh, that makes no difference, Washington being taken by the British, the United States will of course become subject to them, and he, (meaning myself) may as well die now as at any other time, as that will be his fate at all events. I was irritated, and determined that he should not escape with impunity, I immediately replied that I did not believe one word of his information; he retorted somewhat angrily that it was not only taken, but burnt, and added, even were it not, what chance had we to preserve our country, having a sea coast of nearly three thousand miles, without any fortification; the United States, I replied, have the power to fortify the whole line of coast; and to his enquiry, in what manner they could do it, I answered with men and bayonets. I had the pleasure to see him depart in no very enviable humor.

Through the influence of Lieutenant Norris, I was liberated on the evening of the day I arrived at Kingston, in which place I remained but a few days, and then not having liberty to view the navy-yard, and in fact, not being suffered to leave the street in which I boarded, I had no opportunity of seeing any of the curiosities of the place. Between York and Kingston, although a distance of about two hundred miles, I do not recollect having seen one town, either situate on, or in view of the lake.

I was now put on board a boat and ordered to Montreal. After we had got some distance below Kingston, perhaps seventy or eighty miles, near the seven Islands, we met a fleet of boats, one hundred and ten in number, two of which were gun boats, the rest were laden with military stores, cash to pay the troops, and the timbers of a vessel built in England, even to the last pin, and ready to put together, to enable them to maintain their superiority on lake Ontario. After the fleet had passed, I intimated to the officer who commanded the boat I was on board of, that I would be much gratified if he would run his boat on the other side of the St. Lawrence, which he could do with as much facility as upon this—his reply was, I understand you, sir, but were the other side of the river equally near, you could not make your escape, as upon the first attempt, I would have you shot—I bantered him by telling him, that if he would agree to run his boat as near the American shore as he then was to the British, I would execute a bond for five hundred dollars, payable in ten days, in any house in Boston or New York, that he might mention, and he might fire all the guns on board after me, and kill me if he could; but all would not do, neither bribe nor persuasion could induce him to alter his course. I well knew that the guns had lain in the boat until the powder was so damp that it would have been next to a miracle if one amongst them would go off. It was my fixed determination if I could have got near enough, to have made the shore, to have jumped overboard, and run all risks. Had I been then able to have effected my escape, I would have pressed a horse, and made the best of my way to Sackett's harbor, where I would have given information of the fleet of boats, as the whole of them might have been easily taken, and would have been a valuable prize.

On proceeding a little further, we saw a drove of fat bullocks, consisting of one hundred head; which I learned, had been smuggled across, from the state of New-York, at the Seven Islands. The drovers were met that day by the British commissary, who paid them twenty dollars per hundred, for the beef cattle, all in gold. Upon their return down the river, the drovers put up for the night, at the same tavern where I lodged; and, sometime after supper, I walked into the room where they were seated; there were but two of them, and had the gold spread on the table, in the act of dividing it. I that night obtained information of their real names, for they had passed by fictitious ones; and, also learned the name of the town, in which one of them resided, and made a memorandum of the whole, with a view to their apprehension, if I could make my escape. I had also viewed them so particularly, that I would have been able to recognize them any where; but fortunately for them, I was detained in imprisonment until after the peace.

The conditions of my parole having been broken by the enemy, by my imprisonment at Kingston, I, of course, no longer felt myself in honor bound to comply with them; and had been for some time anxiously waiting an opportunity of effecting an escape. I had some thoughts of making the attempt that night, on board a large canoe, that lay a little way down the river from where we had landed, and preparatory to my going down to the boat, where my man Hughes, and another young man who belonged to the boat, and who had agreed to start with me if I got any chance of escape, were awaiting me. I took an opportunity to enter into conversation with one of the smugglers who was standing by the door, and in the course of our talk enquired of him about the pass of the Seven Islands, and whether the Indians who inhabited them, were friendly or hostile; he gave me some little information and after a while turned into the house. I then went down to the boat and had just communicated my views to my friends, when I was called to from the house by Lieutenant Norris; I immediately went up, after having told my men that I would be back as soon as I could get away, and that we should then put out—the night was very dark, and had we once got under weigh, it would have been a difficult matter to re-capture us.

Upon my reaching the house imagine my disappointment when handed into a room by the Lieutenant, who locked the door as soon as we had entered, telling me that he would keep me company, and pointing to a table upon which lay his sword and pistols, gave me to understand that he would kill me, if I made an attempt to escape; he afterwards informed me that one of the smugglers had told him to take care of me, as I would leave him to-night, and that I had been asking about the passes of the Seven Islands. He then entreated me not to make any attempt to leave him, for if I made my escape it would ruin him, as Major Rogers had suspicions about his loyalty, and he believed that I was placed under his care, merely to try his fidelity. He was a clever fellow, and he and his wife had treated me well, and I should have been sorry to have attempted any thing which would have involved him in difficulties. I therefore pledged my word that I would not attempt leaving him, and, for the present gave up my hopes of escape; he however remained with me until morning, when we re-embarked, and proceeded on our voyage. Nothing occurred worth notice, until we came to what was called the ————, down which, though a distance of nine miles, we passed in the short space of fifteen minutes. I saw some Canadians drawing up a boat, which appeared to be a very difficult undertaking—they had a long rope attached to the boat, one end of which was tugged at by twenty or thirty men—hence we proceeded to La Chine, a distance of nine miles from Montreal, where having landed, Lieutenant Norris conducted me to a tavern, and left me with instructions to remain there until his return. In the mean time I called for something to drink, which I procured without difficulty. I then told the landlord that I would want something to eat also, but I could not procure a mouthful. Upon the return of the Lieutenant, I reported my bad success, when he applied with no better fortune. We then proceeded together to all the public houses, and a good many of the private ones; nothing was to be had.

It was then nearly dark and raining, and we had had nothing to eat since morning. He then instructed us to proceed on the road to Montreal, until we could procure something, and accordingly John Hughes, two others who belonged to the boat, and myself put forward on the road. After having travelled about a mile, we came to a good looking stone house, and here I repeated my call for supper, and received for answer, as before, that I could not have any; they could not give us what they had not themselves. The rain still continued, and the darkness had considerably increased; however we dashed through the mud for something like another mile, when we reached another tavern; here we received the same answer as before, and as for lodging, they could not well accommodate us, but we might lie down on the bar-room floor, which was covered with mud; having no alternative we were obliged to accept the offer, and after awhile they procured us some apples and milk, for which they charged us a handsome price; for our lodgings, however, they charged us nothing. We set forward in the morning towards Montreal, and after travelling two or three miles, espied a snug little farm house at some distance from the road; the prospect looked cheering, and we immediately struck off in its direction. The farmer himself, who proved to be a countryman of our own, met us at the door, invited us to walk in, and handed down a decanter of old whiskey, requesting us to help ourselves. When he heard how we had been treated the evening before, and that we had not breakfasted, but would gladly do so with him, unless he should plead poverty as the rest had done; he immediately replied that he would have something prepared for us, and in a few minutes we sat down to as good a breakfast as any man could wish for, and with stomachs well prepared for wreaking ample satisfaction, to atone for previous abstemiousness. Having finished breakfast, we called for the bill, but our hospitable entertainer absolutely refused to receive any recompense, saying that he should be visited with worse times than the present, before he would receive payment for so trifling a service to a fellow countryman.

Nothing deserving notice came under my observation, until we arrived at Montreal, where as we passed along the streets, the citizens crowded their doors and pavements, and pointing to me, cried out, "there goes an American officer he's a d——d pretty creature, isn't he?" I had then been a prisoner nearly three months and was without hat, coat or vest. It was exceedingly mortifying to me to be held up in my present situation as a specimen of American officers, after having been by themselves stripped almost to a state of nudity. I was exceedingly wrath, and had my power been then equal to my will, I would have taken ample vengeance.

From Kingston to Montreal, along the St. Lawrence, there are nine smart little villages, viz.: Prescott, Youngstown, Edwardsburg, Williamsburg, Osnaburg. Cromwell, Dulac, Cidris, Vaudril and La Chine. Some part of the country appeared to be fertile, and there were several handsome farm houses, whose exterior spoke loudly for the comfort of their inhabitants.

Montreal is the capital of an island of the same name, formerly called Villa Marie; it is the second place in Canada for strength, buildings and extent, and besides the advantages of a better climate, for delightfulness of situation, is much preferable to Quebec. It stands on the side of a hill sloping to the south, with many agreeable villas upon it, which, with the island of St. Helen, and the river, which is about two miles broad, forms a most charming landscape. The city is not very broad from north to south, but covers a great deal of ground from east to west, and is nearly as populous as Quebec.

The streets are regular, forming an oblong square, the houses well built, and the public edifices far exceed those of Quebec in beauty and commodiousness; the residence of the knights hospitalers, is extremely magnificent; there are several gardens within the walls, particularly those of the Governor, the Sisters of the Congregation, the Nunnery Hospital, the Recollects, Jesuits Seminary, &c.; there are also many other gardens and plantations without the gates. The churches and religious houses are of the greatest neatness and simplicity. The city has seven gates, but its fortifications are inconsiderable, being encompassed by a slight wall of masonry, sufficient only to prevent a surprise from the numerous tribes of Indians, with whom they are surrounded, and who used to resort in large bodies, to the annual fair, held here from June to the end of August. On the inside of the town, is a cavalier on an artificial eminence, with a parapet, and six or eight guns, called the citadel. The number of inhabitants, I was informed, amounted to about six thousand. The neighboring shores supply them with a vast variety of game in the different seasons, and the island abounds with soft springs, which form many pleasant rivulets.— They drive a considerable trade in furs; and the place is well calculated for commerce, as vessels of two hundred tons burthen can come directly up to the city. It stands one hundred and twenty miles south of Quebec, and one hundred and ten north of Albany. This island formerly belonged to the French, but was taken by generals Amherst and Murray, on the eighth of September, one thousand seven hundred and sixty. By the capitulation, all the French forces were sent to old France, and thus it became subject to the crown of Great-Britain; it was afterwards confirmed to them by the peace of one thousand seven hundred and sixty-three.

After I had been in Montreal a few days, I was given to understand, that a number of American officers had been paroled home from this place, and made application to the provost major for a parole to go home; he would apply to the governor, he said, and if I would call at his office in a day or two, he would inform me of the result. After repeated calls on my part, he enquired upon what terms I expected to be paroled. I told him I would agree not to lift arms, until legally exchanged. He then asked me if I would agree not to lift arms during the war? I replied that it was not fair to ask me to agree to such terms, and that at all events, I could not, nor would not accept of a parole, badly as I liked being a prisoner, upon any such terms. He then informed me that I would not be paroled on any other terms; and so finished the discussion.

A short time afterwards, a chance of escape was offered me by a friend, who promised to procure me a pass, provided I would change my name, and enter with him as a boatman. When I reached the narrows, I could take a canoe and paddle across to the American shore, as he was going up the river with liquor to the British army. This I declined, not liking the idea of changing my name; and it was absolutely necessary for any one who attempted to travel in that country then, to have a pass, as to be found without one, subjected the person to instant arrest, and of course I could not apply for one in my own name, consequently could not avail myself of the opportunity.

While killing time one day in a tavern at Montreal, a deserter from the American army came in, who had a great deal to say about the Americans. To the question of why he deserted, he replied that it was entirely in consequence of the bad treatment he received from his officers. We had some warm words, and I cautioned him to be careful, now that winter was coming on, in case he could not get work to support himself, which it was more than probable would prove the case, not to turn his hand to stealing, as a comrade of his had been hanged but a few days before for an offence of the kind; and it was, I thought, a most excellent plan adopted by the British, to get rid of such rubbish, as no man can place confidence in. It may well be supposed that he did not wait to hear any more.

About this time a man who resided a few miles from town came and told me that if I would give him one hundred dollars, he would deliver me safe in the United States, in the course of one night. Soon after, a gentleman, a resident of Montreal, told me, that if I would disguise myself by putting on a good suit of clothes, he would give me a seat in his calash, procure a pass for me, and carry me in part of a day to where I might conveniently cross in a canoe. Both these offers required money, and I postponed answering for a day or two, hoping that I might be able to raise the money by some exertion. Accordingly I enquired of my landlord, he being an American, whether he could inform me of any means of procuring fifty or one hundred dollars on loan; he recommended me to a mercantile house, which he told me, was immensely rich, and American; the name of the firm was "Ballas and

Gaits," they had made a splendid fortune by smuggling business, carried on between them and some of the merchants of New-York and Boston, who exchanged flour, etc., for dry goods; if I would apply to them, he thought there would be no doubt of my success. In pursuance, therefore, of this advice, I immediately waited upon Mr. Gaits, and after stating my situation to him, told him I had been recommended to apply to his house for the loan of from fifty to one hundred dollars, and that I would pay the amount with any per centage he might demand, to any house in New-York or Boston, in ten days after I should have arrived in the United States. He then enquired if I had made my case known to the British officers, and upon my replying that they were well acquainted with all the circumstances of my situation, remarked that if the gentlemen of the place were made acquainted with my wants, the sum would easily be raised. I told him that although reduced by misfortune to the disagreeable necessity of applying to a stranger, and I expected a gentleman, for a loan of money, I was not yet reduced to beggary, and left him.

About this time Cornet Gillas was brought on, and left at the same house with me; he was a spirited, and had been a very stout young man, but was now much disabled, by rheumatic pains, which I believe he never got entirely rid of. Having been irritated while at Fort George, by being put into the guard-house, among several refractory soldiers, he had commenced beating them with a leg of a bench, which he had broken off, and before the guard alarmed by the cries of "*murder*," had time to come to their assistance, he had knocked down three or four. For this, he was taken and stretched on a log, sunk level with the ground, where he was tightly fastened down with ropes, and kept in that position for several days. It was here he had taken the rheumatic pains, under which he was suffering.

A company of merchants, five in number, from Long Point, and who had come to Montreal to lay in goods, put up at the tavern where I lodged, and sent me an invitation to come to their room after supper, and drink some wine with them. They were very sociable, and made a good many inquiries relative to my imprisonment and subsequent treatment. I gratified them in every particular. Next morning, I was speaking to one of their boatman, who was going to get his watch repaired, and I asked him to show it to me, and to my astonishment he drew out my own watch. It had a compass on the face of it, and the needle being loose, I asked him if he could fasten it, and upon his answering that he could not, I told him to hand it to me, and I would fasten it for him; when he was in the act of reaching it to me, I remarked, that I had carried that watch a much longer time than he, and that it was the very one which had been taken from me by the Indians, when I was made prisoner; he immediately drew back his hand, when I told him not to be alarmed, as I had no notion of laying claim to it, as I supposed *he* came honestly by it. He then handed it to me, when I put in the needle, I showed him the spring which fastened it, and returned it to him, saying, that if I had money I would buy it of him, as it was a favorite watch, and had been the gift of a brother, now dead; but, that as my means had been taken, as well as my watch, I had no means of gratifying myself, by its recovery. The same evening, however, the merchants again sent for me to their room, and after some conversation, and drinking a few glasses of wine, one of them drew out my watch, and presented it to me, saying, he hoped I would receive it as a mark of their friendship, and that they felt very happy in being able to restore it to me. They had each subscribed five dollars. I feel sorry that I cannot recollect the names of men who acted so very generously.

Next morning Gillas and I were ordered to repair to the wharf, there to go aboard a vessel bound for Quebec; previous to going on board, I called to bid Mrs. Norris farewell; she inquired if I had any money to purchase necessaries for the voyage, and upon my replying that I had not, presented me with four dollars, which she insisted upon my taking, regretting, at the same time, the absence of her husband, which disabled her from giving me a much larger sum. We repaired, according to orders, to the wharf, and went aboard of a merchant vessel. I regret very much that the loss of detached parts of my manuscript, has put it out of my power in several instances to mention the names of persons from whom I had received kindnesses; the captain of the vessel which conveyed us to Quebec, is amongst the number of those, whose names it would have afforded me pleasure to record; he was in every sense of the word, a gentleman. He conducted us to his cabin, and opened for us his library, assuring us if we could find any thing in it to divert ourselves, we were perfectly welcome to its use. When dinner time came he sent for us to dine with him, and continued to entertain us at his own table all the time we were aboard; dinner over, he brought in brandy and wine, requesting us to make choice and help ourselves. In the evening, after supper, we had our wine and a pack of cards for our amusement, when he would himself take a hand. This, as the saying is, was too good to last long, and in three days we reached Quebec, a large and handsome town, and the capital of Canada.

The first place taken notice of upon landing here, is a square of an irregular figure, with well built houses on each side, on the back of which is a rock; on the left it is bounded by a small church, and on the right are two rows of handsome, and apparently convenient houses, built parallel to each other. There is another row between the church and the harbor, and another and a large one on the side of the bay. This is a kind of suburb; between this and the great street is a very steep ascent, with steps for foot passengers. This is what is called the Upper Town; the city being divided into an Upper and Lower Town. In the upper is situated the Bishop's palace, a very elegant and splendid building, and between two large squares is a fort, where the Governor lodges. The *Recolects*, a sort of Franciscan friars, have handsome houses over against it. On the right of the Cathedral, and directly facing it, stands the ci-devant Jesuits college. In a direct line from the fort, and parallel to each other, run two streets which are crossed by a third, and between these and the Governor's house are situate a church and a convent. The houses are mostly built of stone, and the number of inhabitants amounted, I was informed, to about seven thousand. The fort is also a handsome building. Quebec is situated at the confluence of the rivers St. Lawrence and St. Charles. The river, which from the sea hither, is about four or five leagues broad, narrows all of a sudden to the breadth of a mile. The harbor is safe and commodious, and the water is about five fathoms deep.

Quebec is not regularly fortified, but it cannot be easily taken, for the harbor is flanked with two bastions, which at high tides are almost level with the water. In the year seventeen hundred and eleven, the British fitted out a fleet, with a design to conquer Canada, which failed, in consequence of the Admiral rashly following his own opinion, although in direct contradiction to the advice of his pilot, in sailing too close to the "Seven Isles," by which piece of imprudence he lost his largest ships, and upwards of three thousand of his best soldiers. On the eighteenth of October, seventeen hundred and fifty-nine, it was taken however, by the British, under the command of General Wolfe, who fell in the battle, after he had the satisfaction of knowing that his troops were victorious.

In December, seventeen hundred and seventy-five, it was attacked by the Americans, under General Montgomery, who was killed, and his army repulsed. Quebec lies three hundred and twelve miles from the sea coast, and five hundred and ninety northwest of Boston.

Having arrived here we were paroled to Beaufort, a village at the distance of about three miles, where we were ordered to proceed immediately. We got into a calash or sort of gig, which carried us there in a short time, for which conveyance we were charged two dollars each. Here we fell into company with a number of paroled officers, and here I again came into company with my old friends and companions, Major Galloway and Captain Roberts from Cumberland county, the latter of whom had been made prisoner at the battle of Bridgewater, on the twenty-fifth of July eighteen hundred and fourteen.

Here also we met with Major Wilson, Major Stauton, Col. Churchill, and several other officers from the state of New-York. The hostages who had been kept in Quebec prison for several months, were also at this place under parole.

The officers whose names I have above mentioned, had been marched to this place over land, under guard, and had been, during their march, treated by the guard with the utmost contempt. When in their passage along the roads, they came in contact with a mud hole, although there might be plenty of room to pass round, they were compelled to walk through it, at the point of the bayonet. In many places they were almost knee deep in mud.

During the whole of the war, the treatment received by the American prisoners, was cruelly mortifying to them, and deeply degrading to the captors. That of an officer belonging to the New-York militia, who had been wounded and made prisoner, was shameful in the extreme: He had been shot through his shoulder, and had his collar-bone broken, so that he could not raise his arm, and it was put into a sling by some of his companions. He was dragged all the way to Montreal without having had his wound dressed, and even in his bloody clothes, a distance of at least fifty miles, where it was dressed; but assistance so long neglected came too late, and the unfortunate man died at Beaufort, totally neglected. I never felt more pity for suffering humanity, than this poor fellow's case excited. Death is at all times a scene of sorrow, even when accompanied by every thing calculated to soothe the mind, and relieve the anxiety of the sufferer; how much more distressing, therefore, must have been the situation of a man dying far from home, in the midst of his enemies, and under the most mortifying treatment, with his thoughts resting on his family, who would be left to lament his loss?

I will mention another instance of unfeeling treatment, towards a private soldier; a musket ball had broken his leg, and in the absence of all other care or attendance, his companions had splintered it up as well as they knew how, and it was beginning to heal. On his way to La Chine, where he was taken by water, he was rudely thrown from the boat by a British soldier, because he did not move as fast as those who were well, and his leg was again broken. He was then hauled in a cart, into which he was brutally tumbled, to Montreal, in a state of extreme suffering.

At Beaufort the officers formed themselves into messes, and rented a room or two, as the mess was larger or smaller. Major Galloway, Stanton, myself and some others, whose names I do not recollect, belonged to Col. Churchill's mess. The Colonel and Major Galloway had each a man to wait on them, who cooked for us. We paid three dollars a week for the room, and the privilege of cooking at the kitchen fire; a cart load of wood cost two dollars, a turkey one dollar, a chicken twenty-five cents, and beef was twenty cents a pound, and by marketing for ourselves, and messing together we fared better and at less cost, than if we were at a boarding house. Capt. Roberts boarded at the only tavern in the place, and from their manner of cooking, which I witnessed one day, I had no desire whatever, to belong to his company. Eels they kept barrelled up as herrings are, and they cook them in a different manner from what I had ever seen before. which is called the French method. The landlady, whom I saw dress them, took a large one out of the barrel, it was just as it had been caught, except that it had been in pickle, and having twisted it around in the form of a ring, tied it in that shape with a piece of thread, when opening the bar-room stove door she hung it on a hook placed inside of the stove, and closing the door left it there. After a while she came back with a plate in her hand, and with a tongs removed the eel, and put it on the plate, when it was conveyed to the table, and the guests commenced carving and helping themselves.

Those who disliked eating the skin, might leave it with the intestines on the plates.

We had the privilege of walking as far as the bridge over the river Montmorency, near which is a beautiful waterfall, formed by the waters of the Montmorency, pouring over steep rocks, and falling with a tremendous noise, into the St. Lawrence, from a distance of from one to two hundred feet.

Major Vandewenter, from Philadelphia, one of the hostages, who had been confined in Quebec Jail, was at that time permitted by the British to act as American agent, the former agent having been sent home some time previous. In making out his requisition to pay for cloathing, &c., he so managed as to have such an overplus, as enabled him to give each of us two months pay, with which I purchased cloathing.

The houses here are principally of stone, two stories high, with very steep roofs; they are built in this manner to facilitate the falling off of the snow, in the winter, which would otherwise injure the roof, as it lies in that season, to the depth of from six to seven feet. The quality of the land, about Beaufort, appears to be good, principally lime stone; the farms are narrow, running in one direction, to the base of a large mountain, and in the other to the water's edge. The people here are excessively fond of onions, you will hardly find a family, who will not lay up for winter use, from fifty to a hundred bushels. They seem to live very poorly, not being able to buy beef on account of its very high price.

I had been here between three and four weeks, when one evening a British officer came in and told us we must make preparations to go on board of a vessel then in harbor and bound for Halifax, on the following evening. We enquired if it would be necessary for us to purchase sea stores, and were told that it would be entirely unnecssary, as we should fare as well as the Admiral. We accordingly went aboard without making any preparations, and were put in possession of a large cabin. The weather was very cold, and it blew quite a gale. That evening the Captain went ashore, and Captain Hunt, from the state of New York, who had previously managed to engage a Frenchman, to pilot him across the country to the United States, in case he should be able to make his escape, commenced preparations; the better to assisst, the Frenchman had hired himself on board in capacity of a waiter; they got out of the cabin window into the boat which lay astern, but to their mortification, found there were no oars; these, after considerable manœuvering we managed to convey from deck into the cabin, one party keeping the guard busy in conversation; from the cabin they were handed to the boat, and having muffled the oars, and being joined by four others, the painter was cut, and notwithstanding there were fifty sail of vessels in the harbor, each one having a lanthorn mounted, and two guards patrolling the deck, they effected their escape, and got safe to land. There still remained on board the vessel, seventeen of our number, so that those who made their escape were not missed until the following morning at nine o'clock, when the Captain came aboard and had the roll called. We were told to prepare to leave the cabin in an hour, and that we should in future take up our quarters in the hold; when we urged that it was rather a hard case to punish us, for the offences of others, our captain told us that he was very well aware that they could not have got away without our assistance. We then stated that it seemed rather like punishing us for not having availed ourselves of the opportunity presented us, as the boat was sufficiently large to hold us all—the only reply he condescended to make us, was, that he would let us know that we had our eldest "*brudder*" aboard, and that he would take care of us—he was a Scotchman by the name of Snowden. When the hour given us for preparation had expired, we were marched into the hold, where we were kept for twenty-one days, three days and nights of which we had nothing to eat, and when at length they did furnish us with provisions, they were of such a quality as an American dog would not eat, without the necessary stimulus of starvation—they consisted of old sea bread or biscuit, which, for any thing I know, was twenty years old, at all events, it was so completely eaten up by the worms, all that the worms could penetrate, the outside part being only left, and that was so hard that it would require a hammer to break it. Bad as it was we were not furnished with more than one fourth of a common soldier's allowance. This was shovelled up into a sack and with a bone of beef thrown into the hold as if to so many dogs. We cut the meat and broke the bread into small pieces, and boiled all together, making a kind of soup called lobscouse; while it was in preparation, we had made each of us a spoon, and this done, it was poured out upon a large wooden dish, and standing round, we played away, until the hollow rattle of our spoons upon the dish reminded us that it was empty. We fared twice a day in this sumptuous manner. The water too which they gave us to drink was most dreadful stuff; no human being could drink it without holding his nose, the stench was so great. In the evening, our waiter had the good fortune to procure us a bucket of water, which was divided amongst us as though it was a luxury, and indeed to our tasting, it was delicious.

When we came to a place called "Ship Harbour,"

the vessels were obliged to lie to for a couple of days, in consequence of bad weather. We had a very heavy sea, and the winds were very rough, and previous to our reaching Ship Harbour, had lost one of the vessels belonging to the fleet, which I believe was never heard of. It must have gone down, as a few days afterwards, the bodies of some of the crew were picked up on shore, where they had been cast, and were recognized by the device and number on their buttons. Fortunately there were no Americans on board of her. Here we were transferred to another vessel, bound to England; after we had been put on board, we were ordered to go below among the sick and invalids—they were then dying fast, and they were every day throwing them overboard; the place too, was very filthy, and full of vermin. We refused to go down, and remained on deck the whole day, which was bitterly cold, and the wind very high. We then petitioned the Admiral for better quarters, than those assigned to us, and declared in the strongest terms that we would otherwise remain on deck until we perished, and we walked the deck from early in the morning until dark, when one of the army officers invited us into their cabin, where they had something prepared for us to eat, which was the first meal we had eaten since we had had our lobscouse the day previous.

Next morning we were ordered back on board of the vessel we had left, and taking advantage of the opportunity offered us by the sailors, some of whom were going ashore, we gave them some money, to purchase for us something to eat. When they returned they brought us a bag of potatoes and some fresh cat-fish, of which we soon cooked a mess, and I thought it was the best meal I had ever eaten. After the storm had somewhat abated we again set sail for Halifax.

The fleet that went down with us, consisted of twenty sail, two of which were seventy-fours; after we had been several days in the hold, the stove was hoisted upon deck, and we were compelled to do without fire for the balance of the passage. Orders had been issued that the lights should be extinguished at eight o'clock, and that the fire in the stove should be drowned out at nine o'clock. In consequence of neglect in this last particular, we suffered this severe privation. The weather was extremely cold, and the ropes were all hanging with ice, besides we could not induce the Captain to sell us any provisions. I offered the cabin boy one dollar for a pint of beef soup, but he refused, saying, that if he gave it, he would get the rope's end—he sold us rum, however, at one dollar per bottle, and it will be readily perceived that we paid our devotions pretty regularly to the bottle, when I state that during the passage we paid him for rum alone, upwards of two hundred dollars. We could not have lived without it, and were forced to "keep our spirits up by pouring spirits down." If our Captain were tired of us, before he took away the stove, we now gave him double cause to be so, as we kept up a continual singing, and noise until ten and eleven o'clock, every night, and very often to a much later hour. He at length became afraid of us, and had his guard doubled, by application to some of the other vessels. He afterwards made another application, and recovered his temper, when strengthened by a couple of army officers. Alarmed as he was, he would have been much more so, had he known that we had actually agreed to take the vessel as soon as we got out of the St. Lawrence, and had sea-room. Our plan was to be put in operation in the night, but unfortunately for us we got into the ocean early in the day, and by night we were inside of the Halifax coasters. We had two midshipmen and one lieutenant of our navy on board, and had so far succeeded as to have made a passage, by which we could at pleasure enter the apartment where the guard slept, and their arms being stacked on the floor, could have seized them when we pleased. Two of the stoutest of us were to go on deck, but two being allowed up at a time, and the stairs of the hatches were to be filled with men, ready to rush up as soon as they should have seized the guard—some were to fasten down the hatches on the sailors, and others to take care of the cabin and the officers. We would then have compelled the sailors to work the vessel into New-York, but when night came on, our lieutenant discouraged the whole undertaking by informing us that we were then inside of the Halifax coasters, and that should we be so fortunate as to escape from the fleet, we would be re-taken by them, and if so, it was as likely as not, we should all be hung to the yard arms, without further comment. Having no particular propensity for *swinging*, we abandoned the project, and landed on the following day at Halifax.

We were marched up the street, under guard like a parcel of felons, to the office of the Provost Major, where we received paroles to Prescott, a village across the bay from Halifax, and were marched back in the same order to the boat; cheered as we went along by the expression of sympathy, from the by-standers—ah! poor devils! exclaimed a poor old Irish woman; in the fulness of her heart and the roughness of her phraseology, she expressed her pity for our desolate situation, and I have no doubt she felt for us from her soul, for her manner indicated sincerity and her eye glistened with a tear. We were put on board with our little store of baggage, and in the morning landed at Prescott, our place of parole.

About the time I went on shore I was taken very ill, indeed I had been in a very weak state of health, ever since I had had the fever, and my treatment from that time was not such as to strengthen or improve it. I remained unwell for several days, and wrote to Halifax for medical aid, asking even as a favor, to go to the hospital, and received neither medical assistance, nor answer of any kind. I took a fancy to a drink of cider, and accordingly went to a tavern, where I got some very good; it appeared to do me good, and I continued the operation, and recovered, without other medicine.

Halifax is the capital of Nova Scotia, and was founded in the year seventeen hundred and forty-nine with a view to secure the British settlements from the French and Indians. It was divided into thirty-five squares, each containing sixteen lots of forty by sixty feet.— They have one established church, and one meeting house. The city is surrounded by picketings, and guarded by forts on the outside, and has since been very strongly fortified. Along the Chebucto, south of the town, are buildings and fish flakes, for a distance of at least two miles, if not more, and on the north of the river they extend for a mile and upwards. The plan was originally contrived, and afterwards considerably improved by the Earl of Halifax. In March of the year seventeen hundred and forty-nine, was first issued the proclamation for the establishment of this settlement, and so favorable were the terms offered to settlers, and so strong the desire of emigration amongst the people, that but two months afterwards, that is to say, in the month of May, persons had offered themselves, to the number of three thousand seven hundred and fifty. They accordingly embarked, and after a prosperous voyage, established themselves in the bay of Chebucto, where they founded their city, calling it Halifax, in honor of their patron.

So actively and with such spirit did they enter into operations. that before the end of October three hundred comfortable wooden houses were built, and as many more during the winter. The British government, too, evinced great liberality in the manner, in which for six successive years, they granted them large supplies of money, for instance, in the year seventeen hundred and forty-nine, they voted them 40,000*l* for their expences; in seventeen hundred and fifty they granted them *l*57,582 17*s* 3*d* 1-4; in seventeen hundred and fifty-one, *l*53,927 14*s* 4*d*; in seventeen hundred and fifty-two, a sum of *l*61,492 19*s* 4*d* 1-4; in seventeen hundred and fifty-three, *l*94,615 12*s* 4*d*; in seventeen hundred and fifty-four, *l*55,447 2*s*; and in seventeen hundred and fifty-five, *l*49,418 7*s* 8*d*. This city has at length attained a degree of splendor, that bids fair to rival the first cities in the United States, for which it has been equally indebted to the late war, to the great increase of population from the influx of exiled loyalists, and to the fostering care of Great-Britain. The harbour is perfectly sheltered from all winds, being at the distance of twelve miles from the sea, and is so spacious that one thousand ships may ride in it without the least danger. Upon it are many commodious wharves which have from twelve to eighteen feet of water at all tides; the streets are regularly laid out, and cross each other at right angles, the whole rising gradually upon the side of a hill, whose top is regularly and very strongly fortified. Many considerable merchants reside in this place, and are possessed of shipping to the amount of several thousand tons, employed in a flourishing trade with Europe, and the West Indies. There is a small, but excellent careening yard for ships of the royal navy, that may come in to refit, and take water, fuel, or provisions on board, in their passage to, and from the West Indies. It is well provided with naval stores; and ships of the line are hove down and repaired with the greatest ease and safety. Several batteries of heavy cannon, command the harbour, particularly, those upon George's island, which being very steep and high, and situated in mid channel, is well calculated to annoy vessels, in any direction. Above the careening yard, which is at the upper end of the town, there is a large basin, or piece of water, communicating with the harbor below, is nearly twenty miles in circumference, and capable of containing the whole navy of England; it is entirely sheltered from all winds, and has but one narrow entrance, which leads into the harbor. There are many detached settlements, formed by the loyalists, along the basin; the lands at a small distance from the water, being generally supposed to be better than those near Halifax. An elegant building is erected near the town, for the convalescence of the navy; but the healthiness of the climate has, as yet, prevented many persons from becoming patients; scarcely any ships in the world, being so free from complaints of every kind in regard to health, as those that are employed upon this station. There is a good light-house, standing upon a small elevation, just off the entrance of the harbor, which is visible, either by night or day, from a distance of six or seven leagues. Halifax is seven hundred and eighty-nine miles north-east of New-York. In winter, the climate is very severe, and much addicted to fogs—but to return to our narrative.

We remained in this place until after the declaration of peace, and boarded during the time we remained, at the different taverns, at an expence of from five to seven dollars a week. Our fare, too, was very poor; breakfast consisted of bread and butter with some roasted herrings, and water, colored with coffee; for dinner they gave us generally a leg of mutton stuffed, and roasted, and plum-pudding—sometimes they would regale us with a roasted goose, but on Fridays we regularly sat down to codfish and potatoes; our suppers were light, consisting of bread slightly marked with butter, and a cup of tea, no doubt, through fear of injuring our digestion. The naval officers were paroled to a small village some miles distant, as they did not like to have them so near the water.

In some parts of Upper Canada, through which I passed, the people did not appear to pay the least respect to the Sabbath day. I have frequently seen women churning butter and baking bread, and men chopping wood, and attending to divers other employments, the same as on week-days. They have a substitute for coffee, of which it has fallen to my lot, more than once to partake, viz.: dry crusts of bread put on the fire and burnt black, then pounded fine, and boiling water being poured upon it, it is suffered to rest for a while when it is pronounced fit for use. Provisions of all sorts were very scarce and dear. In the markets of Halifax, beef was upwards of twenty cents a pound, turkey was fifty cents per lb., wheaten meal, though sour, was twenty-four dollars per barrel, and I saw them manufacturing flour in a mill near Halifax, that was so much spoiled, and so firmly cemented together, that they had to dig it out of the barrel with a heavy spade, it was then placed under a sort of pounder, and after it had been pounded and bolted, through a cross-bolt, the lumps were collected, and after having undergone a repitition of the process, the whole was mixed with fresh wheat, and re-bolted, until made fine enough to pass through, when it was packed and sent to market. Major Galloway and I paid two dollars, at a tavern in Halifax, for a couple of glasses of brandy each, and some oysters, which were so bad, we were forced to leave them untouched.

There were but few men in the village in which we were paroled, some followed. fishing, some the sea, and others the army. The soil of the country around appeared to be very poor, the country abounded with small lakes; the timber was principally scrubby white pine, not growing thicker than from six to twelve inches in circumference. This was the wood used for firing by the inhabitants, each of whom cut and hauled as much as he pleased without interruption. The corn stalks which I saw in some gardens, and this was the only place in which I saw any, were no larger than a person's finger.

About this time the news of the defeat of the British before New-Orleans, reached Halifax, and disappointment and chagrin were depicted in the countenance of every individual, with the exception of the American prisoners, whose joy was almost without bounds. The merchants who had been speculating, and many of them had embarked largely in purchasing the soldiers rights of plunder at New-Orleans, of cotton, sugar, tobacco, &c., were actually thunderstruck. Many of them upon hearing the news, collected all the cash they could lay their hands upon, and disposed of as much merchandise as possible, and cleared out, well knowing that they had not the slightest chance of anything but absolute poverty, if they remained. Every day while I remained there, I witnessed sales of their goods at auction in the streets.

When the news of the victory reached us at Prescott, the officers assembled at what was called "*Jack-*

*son's Tavern,*" where Major Galloway, Captain Crowninshield, myself, and several others boarded, and spent the afternoon in jollity and mirth. "Hail Columbia," I suppose was never sung with more heart-felt gratitude, than we sang it that afternoon; joining hands, forming a circle and walking round, we sang with all our force, disregardful entirely of consequences; but we were permitted to enjoy ourselves without molestation, as there was not a British officer or soldier then resident in the village. Captain Crowninshield had been detained in imprisonment for something like a year after he had been legally exchanged; immediately after the news of peace had reached them, Captain Cushet, the provost Major, sent a line to him, with directions to have his baggage put on board of a certain vessel then lying in the harbor, bound for the United States, and then to repair to his office in Halifax; the Captain did so, and on appearing in the office, the Major asked him if he did not feel rejoiced at the prospect of returning to his family. Crowninshield replied that he did; but added at the same time, "without considering myself at all indebted to you, Captain Cushet." Cushet answered, that thanks were not only due to himself but to several others, gentlemen resident in Halifax, who had interested themselves considerably, to procure his liberation—to this our friend replied, that these of his friends in Halifax, who had interested themselves for him, he did indeed feel deeply indebted, but to Captain Cushet he again asserted he did not conceive himself at all indebted, as he had it in his power to prove without leaving the city, in black and white, that it was through his means alone he had been so long illegally detained in captivity; and he had yet to learn that cruelty and injustice had power to bind the object upon whom they had been practised, to feelings of regard or consideration for his oppressor. This charge was denied most positively and as positively and firmly repeated, when at length, Cushet completely losing all command of his temper, the following dialogue ensued: "You shall not go home even now, sir." "Thank you, sir." "Go on board and remove your baggage, and return to your place of parole." "Thank you, sir." "I will send you to Mellville prison, sir." "Thank you, sir." "Begone out of my office, sir." "Thank you, sir." Captain Crowninshield then left the office and related the circumstance at dinner, when he was warmly greeted by all for his firmness, and they actually carried him on their shoulders round the room. He then called for wine, to treat his fellow officers of whom there were about a dozen, then in the house; we devoted ourselves to merriment and had a jovial time of it; several other paroled American officers gathered in, and before we had retired to rest ourselves, we had consigned to rest upwards of forty bottles of good wine, thus celebrating our country's glory, and our enemies' disgrace, under their very noses. The next morning the Captain made it known that he expected a guard to be sent to conduct him to Melville prison; several of the officers, unknown to him, met together and formed a resolution to attempt his rescue, and if possible prevent his going to jail; he however came to the knowledge of the matter by some means, and begged of them to desist from their purpose, as it was impossibe to prevent his going to jail in an enemy's country; that they would only risk their own lives, without doing him any service; I saw him plead with them, with tears in his eyes, so overcome was he by his feelings, before he could persuade them to give up their project—he, however, at length succeeded; he was so universal a favorite amongst the officers, that I firmly believe, had they after reflection, found the undertaking feasible, they would never have consented to abandon the enterprise.

Captain C. was from Salem, in the state of Massachusetts; he had formerly been the captain of a vessel, which occupation he had followed for nearly twenty years; and was well acquainted with the merchants of Halifax. For some time previous to the war, he had not gone to sea, and would not have again resumed the service, had he not had two vessels laden with goods, captured and run into British ports, where they were condemned under pretence of having smuggled goods aboard. One of the vessels thus captured had a cargo of West India goods, worth ten thousand dollars. Having still something of his property left, he fitted up a small vessel with a swivel gun and a good crew, and went out privateering; he had married a young wife about a year before he went to sea. In his first trip he was fortunate, taking several British vessels; when they proved to be of small value, the valuable part of the cargo was taken out, and she was scuttled; her crew would then be paroled and put on shore—he made, however, two very valuable prizes, one of which sold for one hundred thousand dollars, which served in part to remunerate him for previous losses.

Upon his scond trip, having taken and scuttled two or three vessels, the crews of which not having an opportunity of being put ashore, were still on board, he was on the look-out for an old West Indiaman, bound for Halifax, having a valuable cargo, and which was hourly expected, and when within a short distance of the Halifax coast, came in sight of an old seventy-four; this he mistook for his expected prize, and accordingly made sail for her, and it being late in the evening, and a thick fog, he had got alongside before he discovered his error. Those on board the seventy-four, with a view of correcting his mistake, shoved out their guns, and gave him a broadside; by dint of several times shifting his course, he however, made his escape, and ran on until he thought himself safe, when he lay too, fearful that if he proceeded he would get out of the track of the West Indiaman; unfortunately for him however, his antagonist had shaped her course in the same manner, and was alongside before day-break of the following morning, when before he could get away, she poured into him a broadside, which shot off his main-mast, and otherwise so far disabled him as to preclude all possibility of escape—he consequently struck his flag, and was fired into even after that process. When taken, he had twice as many prisoners, as he had of his own crew—they were all taken to Halifax, where they were detained until after the peace.

According to Captain Crowninshield's expectations, in one or two days after he had returned to his place of parole, Captain Cushet came over to pay us, what we called in derision, our starvation money, more properly, subsistence money, being twenty dollars per month, in lieu of rations, which was nothing like sufficient to support us; he had a guard with him, and told Crowninshield that he must now set out for Melville prison. In conversation which they held about the matter, and in reply to the question of why he should be sent to prison, the captain was informed that it was not for anything he had said, but solely for the tone in which it had been spoken; he was then taken off, and carried to Melville, where they kept him for about ten days, when he was set at liberty and sent home to Salem. In Melville prison there were confined from twelve to fourteen hundred Americans, who were treated with as much barbarity, as though the worst of convicts, some of them being half naked. John Hughes, one of my men who was confined there, got an opportunity of writing to me, stating how much he suffered from want of clothes and tobacco, at the time I received his letter, I had but two dollars and three shirts which, however, I divided with him, giving him one dollar, and one shirt and a great coat, which proved to him of considerable service.

Melville prison is two hundred feet in length, and fifty broad, it is two stories high, the upper one being for officers, and for the infirmary and dispensary, while the lower part is divided into two prisons, one of which was occupied by French, and the other by Americans. The prison yard covers a space of ground of about one acre in extent, the whole island containing little more than five acres; it is connected on the south side with the main land, by a bridge. In a journal which has fallen into my hands, I find a very minute account of the prison on Melville Island and the treatment of the unfortunate men confined there, which I copy in order to show my readers, that I am not the only one who speaks hastily of our English captives. With the language or sentiments of the writer I have nothing to do, and merely copy it as confirming my own statement, as to the hardships suffered by the inmates of the prison, and as giving a more minute account of its discipline and regulations, than I was enabled to procure from enquiry. The writer of the journal referred to, went from the Port of Salem, as assistant surgeon, on board a privateer, in December of 1812—the title page of the work is lost, and I am consequently unable to give his name.

"As to the inside of the prison at Melville, if the American reader expects to hear it represented as a place resembling the large prisons for criminals in the United States, such as those at Boston, New York, or Philadelphia, he will be sadly disappointed. Some of these prisons are as clean, and nearly as comfortable as some of the monasteries and convents on the continent of Europe. Our new prisons in the United States, reflect great honor on the nation, they speak loudly that we are a considerate and humane people; whereas the prison at Halifax, erected solely for the safe keeping of prisoners of war, resembles a horse stable with stalls or stancheons for separating the cattle from each other. It is to a contrivance of this sort that they attach the cords that support those canvass bags or cradles, called hammocks. Four tiers of these hanging nets were made to swing one above the other, between these stalls or stancheons. To those unused to such lofty sleeping berths, they were rather unpleasant situations for repose. But use makes every thing easy.

The first time that I was shut up for the night in this prison, it distressed me too much to close my eyes. Its closeness and smell were, in a degree, disagreeable, but this was trifling to what I experienced afterwards in another place. The general hum and confused noise from almost every hammock, was at first very distressing. Some would be lamenting their hard fate at being shut up like negro slaves in a guinea ship, or like fowls in a hen-coop, for no crime, but for fighting the battles of their country. Some were cursing and execrating their oppressors; others late at night were relating their adventures to a new prisoner, others lamenting their aberrations from rectitude, and disobedience to parents, and head-strong wilfulness, that drove them to sea contrary to their parents' wish; while others of the younger class were sobbing out their lamentations at the thoughts of what their mothers and sisters suffered, after knowing of their imprisonment. Not unfrequently the whole night was spent in that way, and when about day-break, the weary prisoner fell into a dose, he was waked from his slumber by the grinding noise of the locks, and the unbarring of the doors, with the cry of "turn out—all out," when each man took down his hammock, and lashed it up and slung it on his back, and was ready to answer to the roll call of the turnkey. If any, through natural heaviness, or indisposition, was dilatory, he was sure to feel the bayonet of the soldier, who appeared to us to have a natural antipathy to a sailor, and from what I observed, I believe that in general little or no love is lost between them.

This prison is swept out twice a week by the prisoners. The task is performed by the respective messes in turns. When the prison is washed, the prisoners are kept out until it is perfectly dry. This in the wet seasons, and the severity of winter is sometimes very distressing and dangerous to health; for there is no retiring place for shelter, it is like a stable where the cattle are either under cover or exposed to the weather, be it ever so inclement.

When we arrived here in May 1813, there were about nine hundred prisoners, but many had died by the severity of the winter, and the quantity of fuel allowed by the British government was insufficient to convey warmth through the prison. The men were cruelly harassed by the custom of mustering and parading them in the severest cold, and even in snow storms. The agent, *Miller*, might have alleviated the sufferings of our people, had he been so disposed, without relaxation of duty. But he as well as the turnkey, named *Grant*, seemed to take delight in tormenting the Americans. This man would often keep the prisoners out for many hours, in the severest weather, when the mercury was ten and fifteen degrees below O; under a pretext that the prison had been washed, and was not sufficiently dry for their reception, when, in fact every drop of water used, was in a moment, ice. People in the Southern states, and the inhabitants of England and Ireland, can form no adequate idea of the frightful climate of Nova Scotia. The description of the sufferings of our poor fellows, the past winter, was enough to make one's heart ache, and to rouse our indignation against the agents in this business.

Our people are sensible to kind treatment, and are ready to acknowledge humane and considerate conduct towards themselves or towards their companions, but they are resentful in proportion as they are grateful. They speak very general of the conduct of Miller, the agent, and Grant, the turnkey, with disgust and resentment. A complaint was made to him of the badness of the beef served out to the prisoners, upon which he collected them together, mounted the stair case and began a most passionate harangue, declaring that the beef was good enough and a d——d deal better than they had in their own country; and if they did not eat it, they should have none. He then went on as follows:—Hundreds of you, d——d scoundrels, have been to me begging and pleading, that I would interpose my influence that you might be the first to be exchanged, to return home to your families, who were starving in your absence, and now you have the impudence to tell me to my face, that the king's beef is not good enough for your dainty stomachs. Why some of that there beef is good enough for me to eat. You are a set of mean rascals, you beg of an enemy the favors which your own government won't grant you. You complain of ill treatment, when you never had better in your lives. Had you been in a French prison and fed on horse beef, you would have some grounds of complaint, but here in his Brittannic majesty's royal prison you have everything that is right and proper for persons taken fighting against his crown and dignity.—There is a surgeon here for you, if you are sick, and physic to take if you are sick, and a hospital to go to into the bargain, and if you die, there are boards enough, (pointing to a pile of lumber in the yard) for to make your coffins, and one hundred and fifty acres of land to bury you in, and if you are not satisfied with all this, you may die and be d——d! Having finished this eloquent harangue, orator Miller descended from his rostrum, and strutted out of the prison yard, accompanied with hisses from some of the prisoners.

On a re-examination, however, of the "king's beef," some pieces were found too much tainted for a dog to eat, and the prisoners threw it over the pickets. After this the supply of wholesome meat was such as it ought be, full good enough for Mr. Miller himself to eat, and some of the very best pieces good enough for Mr. Grant, the turnkey.

In all this business of provision for prisoners of war, one thing ought to be taken into consideration, which may be offered as an extenuation of crime alleged against the British agents for prisoners; and that is, that the American solder and sailor live infinitely better in America, than the same class of people do in Great Britain and Ireland. Generally speaking, an American eats three times the quantity of animal food that falls to the share of the same class of people in England, Holland, Germany, Denmark or Sweden.—He sleeps more comfortably, and lives in greater plenty of fish, flesh, vegetables, and spirituous liquors. Add to this, his freedom is in a manner unbounded. He speaks his mind to any man. If he thinks he is wronged, he seeks redress with confidence; if he is insulted he resents it, and if you should venture to strike him, he never will rest quiet under the dishonor; yet you seldom hear of quarrels ending in murder; the dagger and pistol are weapons in a manner unknown; the fist a la mode de John Bull, is commonly the ultimatum of a Yankee's rage.

We often hear the British if they are unsuccessful, lamenting the war between England and America; they call it an unhappy strife between brethren, and they attribute this "unnatural war" to a French influence, and their friends in New England, who are denominated tories, use the same language; they say that all the odium of the war ought to fall on our administration, and their wicked seducers, the French; and yet you will find that both in England and at Halifax, the French meet with better treatment than their dear brothers the Americans.

We found that there were about two hundred French prisoners in Nova Scotia. Some had been there ever since eighteen hundred and three; few of them were confined in prison. The chief of them lived in or near the town of Halifax, working for the inhabitants, or teaching dancing or fencing, or their own language. Some were employed as butchers and cooks, others as nurses in the hospital, and they were every where favored for their complaisance, obedience, and good humor. They had the character of behaving better towards the British officers and inhabitants than the Americans, and I believe, with reason; for our men seem to take delight in plaguing, embarrassing and alarming those who were set over them. A Frenchman always tried to please, while many Americans seemed to take an equal delight in letting their masters know, that they longed to be at liberty to fight them again. I confess I do not wonder, that the submissive, smiling Frenchman made more friends at Halifax, than the ordinary run of American seaman, who seemed too often to look and speak, as if they longed to try again the tug of war, with John Bull.

The daily allowance of the British government to our prisoners, is one pound of bread, one pound of beef, and one gill of peas. Over and above this, we received from the American agent, a sufficiency of coffee, sugar, potatoes and tobacco. The first may be called the bare necessaries of life, but the latter contribute much to its comfortable enjoyment. Whether the British government ought not to have found the whole I am not prepared to determine, but certainly before this addition from our own agent, our men complained bitterly.

We were one day not a little shocked by the arrival of a number of American soldiers who were entrapped and taken with Col. Bœrstler, in Upper Canada. They exhibited a picture of misery, woe and despair. Their miserable condition called forth our sympathy and compassion, and I may add, excited our resentment against the authors of their distress. These unfortunate landsmen had never been used to rough it like sailors, but had lived the easy life of farmers and mechanics. Some of them had never experienced the hardships of a soldier's life, but were raw, inexperienced militiamen. They were taken at some creek, between Fort George and Little York, by the British and their allies. the Indians, who stripped them of most of their cloathing, and then wore them down by long and harassing marches: first to Montreal and then to Quebec, and soon after crowded them on board transports like negroes, in a guinea ship, when some suffered death, and others merely escaped it. It appears from their account, and from every other account, that the treatment of these poor fellows at their capture and on their march, and more especially on board the transports from Quebec to Halifax, was barbarous in the extreme, and highly disgraceful to the British name and nation.

We have asserted uniformly that the prisoners who came from Quebec to Halifax, and Boston, down the St. Lawrence, were treated and provided for in a manner little above brutes. Colonel Scott, now Major Gen. Scott, came by that route from Quebec to Boston, and it is well-known that he complained, that there was neither accommodations, provisions or anything on board the ship, proper for a gentleman. He spoke of the whole treatment he received, with deep disgust and pointed resentment. If an officer of his rank and accomplishments had so much reason for complaint, we may easily conceive what the private soldier must endure.

We paid every attention in our power to these poor fellows, whose emaciated appearance and dejection gave us reason to expect that an end would soon be put to their sufferings by death. They, however, recruited fast, and we were soon convinced that they were reduced to the condition we saw them in, absolutely for want of food. The account which these soldiers gave of their hardships, was enough to fill with rage and resentment the heart of a saint. Four men were not allowed more provisions than what was needful for one. They assured us that if they had not secretly come at some bags of ship bread, unknown to the officers of the transport, they must have perished for want of food.— We cannot pass over one anecdote; some fish were caught by our own people on the passage, in common with the crew, but they were compelled to deliver them all to the captain of the ship, who withheld them from the American prisoners. Some of the prisoners had a little money, and the captain of the transport was mean enough to take a dollar for a single cod-fish, from men in their situation. This fact has appeared in several Boston papers, with the names of the persons concerned, and has never been contradicted or doubted. We give this as the common report, and as the Boston news-papers circulated freely through Nova Scotia and Canada, we infer that had the story been void of truth it would have been contradicted.

About the month of August, Halifax was alarmed, by a report that the prisoners in Mellville jail, had attempted to break prison with a view of seizing upon the town—the report was in some measure correct, as an attempt of the kind had been made, but failed, in consequence of the imprudence of some of the prisoners, who having mined under the wall, crept out in day light to see how it looked from the outside, and being discovered by the guard were fired upon. Whether there was just cause for the extraordinary excitement created by this affair, or any real necessity for the very formidable precautions which were taken, remains a matter of speculation ; be that as it may, however, orders were issued that all loyal citizens should hold themselves in readiness at a moment's warning, to repel the attack of about one thousand unarmed prisoners ; a company of artillery with two pieces of cannon were placed upon an eminence south of the prison, cannons were also placed in different directions so as to play upon the prison, and a line of sentries were placed at regular distances, all the way into the town of Halifax, the people had been actually made to believe that they had sworn to murder every man, woman and child in the town.

The weather was at this time very severe; I have seen many of the American prisoners, with their ears frostbitten, and many of the negroes, who were carried away from their masters, in the United States, actually perished with the cold. The Indians were wrapped up in blankets, feet and legs, and also appeared pretty well preserved with smoke. They came into the town of Halifax about ten or eleven o'clock every day, apparently half frozen, and would mope about the streets from store to store, in search of empty whiskey barrels; when they found one they would take it to the pump, pour water in it, and after rinsing it well, would drink the water; they were the most wretched and pitiable objects I ever saw.

We got through the winter as well as we could, and near the last of February, our ears were blessed with the news of peace, and we immediately commenced making preparations for our return home. According to the articles of the treaty of peace, every officer was bound to pay his debts before he could return home, and Colonel Cushet made a loan, for all the volunteer officers who were there. The only place at which he could raise money, was from a merchant tailor, who bound him to take as much cloathing as would amount to the sum wanted in cash, at his own price, paying the whole to a certain house in Boston in ten days, with ten per cent for the use of it. Having procured cash, we settled our affairs, laid in sea stores, and went aboard—here again the weather seemed to have conspired against us, and we were, in consequence of contrary winds, detained ten days on board; at the expiration of which time we landed at Salem, where we were warmly received by an old friend, Capt. Crowninshield, who had landed a few days previous. He was accompanied by several gentlemen of distinction, who were awaiting our landing on the shore. We proceeded with them to a tavern, where we remained until evening, and then, with a number of the citizens, repaired by invitation to the house of Captain Crowninshield, where we were entertained in the most hospitable manner.

Next morning we took the stage for Boston, and arrived there in time for dinner. We then called upon the paymaster, to have our accounts settled; he told us he had no money, but he would give us due bills, and we could sell them to the brokers, which he did, informing us at the same time where we could get them cashed; we were compelled, however, to allow a discount of twenty per cent.; as we had to pay our borrowed money, we had no other resource—some were forced to allow twenty-five per cent. I took some Philadelphia paper, and when I went to pay my stage fare, they deducted five per cent more—thus, calculating the ten per cent which we paid at Halifax for borrowed money, twenty per cent discount for cash at Boston, and five per cent deducted by the stage proprietor, made in all, an allowance of thirty five per cent which we were compelled to pay. Having at length settled our affairs, we proceeded homeward, passing through New-York and Philadelphia, in each of which places we remained a couple of days. We were compelled to hire horses at Harrisburg, as the stage went no further, and when we arrived at Carlisle, we were detained by the inhabitants, to partake of a dinner prepared for us at the Carlisle tavern—the next day I arrived home in Adams County.

# DESCRIPTION

OF

# UPPER CANADA.

THE province of Upper Canada extends along the northern bank of the river St. Lawrence, the lakes Ontario and Erie, and the water communication from lake Superior, about seven hundred miles, and is five hundred miles wide, according to an imaginary line that divides it from New Britain on the north. The line that divides it from the lower province, begins in lat. 45, at lake Francisco, and takes a due north course to the Outtaways river, then up that river a north west direction to lake Tomiscauting, then due north to the line of New Britain.

The upper province is divided from the United States by a line commencing some distance above the St. Regis village of Indians, situate about seventy-five miles below Ogdensburgh, and running through the centre of the St. Lawrence, to where lake Ontario begins, thence through the centre of it to the outlet of lake Erie, then through the centre of the outlet to the beginning of the said lake, then through the middle of it to the head, and so onward, passing through lakes St. Clair, Huron, Superior, and lake of the Woods; it then takes a south-westerly course to Red Lake, near the headwaters of the river Mississippi.

In the upper province there are no mountains, and but few hills of any considerable height; the country, however, is not of a clear level, but affords sufficient eminences to render it agreeable to the eye, and convenient for the building of water-works, &c.

The sudden rise of ground dividing the waters of lake Erie from lake Ontario, towers in some places five hundred feet high, and almost perpendicular; in general, however, the height does not exceed two hundred feet, and the ascent is very gradual, with natural offsets about five hundred yards wide, upon which are situate plantations, and from which, especially those on the top, are most extensive and beautiful prospects; the eye rests with admiration on the fertile plains below, and lake Ontario stands entirely exposed to observation. Upon the top of this eminence, the country is level, fertile and extremely beautiful; nearly all the waters on the south side of the slope run into lake Erie, though there are but few that find their way through, affording excellent situations for the erection of mills or other buildings requiring water power.

The soil of the province of Upper Canada is exceedingly good in every part, yet it is much the best in the upper part, west south west of the head of the bay Quantic, around the north shore and head of lake Ontario, and the west side of Grand River, in the London District. The lower part of the province is sand and clay mixed; from the head of the bay Quantic, to the head of lake Ontario, it is altogether a black light, rich mould in most places, seven inches deep, after which it is brown clay. On the Grand River, or Indian Land, and in the London District, the soil is sand, brown loam and clay.

The timber of the lower part of the province is chiefly hemlock, birch and beech; that of the middle part, beech, sugar maple and white pine. On the west of the Grand River, the chief of the timber is white pine, elm, bass, black walnut, and the different oaks, chestnut and the like—Indeed in this part of the province, may be found nearly all the varieties of the United States; also, some of the trees of the Balm of Gilead; one of a majestic appearance stands upon the main road, about twenty-five miles west of Niagara. In the lower part of the province, there is but little of any kind of wild fruit, but in the middle part there are several sorts, particularly whortleberries and rice. In the western part there is a great variety of wild fruits, viz.: cranberries, raspberries, grapes, blackberries, and wild potatoes; also, strawberries and plumbs of an excellent quality, and a great quantity of the very best crab apples, which are preserved by the inhabitants with the molasses of pumpkins.

Considerable quantities of wheat are raised in the lower part of the province; and in the middle part, wheat, rye, oats, peas, flax, hemp and corn. In the western part, the product is wheat, which thrives much better here than in any other part; rye, oats and corn, also come to great perfection, as likewise buck-wheat. All kinds of roots and vegetables flourish well in any part of the province, but especially in the west.

All kinds of birds found in the United States are plenty; here is also found a kind of bird, having the same motion and voice as the parakite, so plenty in the state of Kentucky—it differs, however, in colour, being grey, and is called by some, the frolic. Wild ducks are very plenty in all the lakes, as are also geese in all the lakes north of the settlements.

There are seven lakes of considerable size, in the inhabited part of the province, and many parts of the wilderness. Lake Ontario is about two hundred and thirty miles long, from north-east to south-west, and eighty wide about the middle, being of an oval form; it is exceeding deep and in most places appears to be without bottom, as there has been great length of cord let down without finding any. The water is very clear and cool at all times of the year, having the appearance of a large spring. This lake never freezes, except near the shore, where it is shallow, nor does it freeze even there, except in very severe weather, and then only for a very few weeks.

The little lake, or Burlington bay, lies to the south-west of lake Ontario, and is divided from it by a causeway five miles long, and in many places three hundred yards wide; the surface of this causeway is completely level, of a light sand, matted over with grass, and beautifully decorated with groves of timber, chiefly oak, of a middle size, but of an endless variety of curious forms; some six feet in circumference at the butt, yet not more than twelve feet high, with extensive limbs, crooking and twining in all directions. A great number of these trees are entirely encircled with grape vines, and produce great quanties of grapes, of an excellent quality; this lake is about twenty miles in circumference, and generally shallow.

Near the head of bay Quantie, on the north side is a lake of considerable extent, named Hog lake, as also several others not far distant. About twenty miles west of the head of bay Quantie, and fifteen miles north of the shore of lake Ontario, is situated what is called Rice lake, in consequence of the large quantities of rice which grows in it. This lake is from three to nine miles wide, and thirty-six in length, though not very deep. Its course is from east to west; the west end is not far from lake Simcoe. At the east end there is a fall of eighteen feet perpendicular, in the form of a half moon. Below the falls, begins what is called the river Trent, which is tolerably large, and affords many falls fit for water works. It empties into the bay Quantie at the head. This lake communicates with a chain of small lakes, called the Shallow lakes, which also afford rice, and extends near the north end of lake Simcoe. Lake Simcoe lies still west of Rice lake, and is something larger; it communicates with lake Huron to the south-west, by the river Severn.

Lake Erie lies thirty miles distant from lake Ontario, and is three hundred miles long, and from twenty to forty miles wide. This lake is elevated about three hundred feet higher than lake Ontario, which* causes the Falls of Niagara. The water, though pure, is not deep, nor is so safe for navigation as lake Ontario.

The lake St. Clair is situate in a north-westerly course from lake Erie; still further to the north-west is lake Huron, in lat. 42; it is one hundred miles in circumference. From lake Huron to the straits of St. Mary, it is seventy miles to lake Superior, which is fifteen hundred miles in circumference, and lies between forty-six and fifty degrees N. latitude, and between eighty-four and ninety degrees west longitude from London. The island Royal, situate near the middle of this lake is one hundred miles long, and forty wide.

This province also contains many fine streams of water, the principal of which are the following:

The Ottaways, or, as it is sometimes called, Grand River, is a large stream, rising out of lake Tomiscauting, and running a south-easterly course, and empties itself in the St. Lawrence, above and below Montreal. The spring floods in the river rise in the month of June, or thereabout, and are often very destructive to the young crops. There is a great variety of fish in this river,

The river Cananocqua is also a considerable stream, and empties into the St. Laurence a few miles below Kingston.

There is a stream of some note, called Myre's creek, which is said to abound with fish; the water is remarkably pure and clear; it empties into the bay Quantie about fifty miles north of Kingston.

The river Trent also empties into the head of bay Quantie from Rice lake, is large, and contains a variety of fish; many hundred barrels of salmon are caught in this stream every fall.

Duffer's creek is also a fine stream, emptying into lake Ontario, thirty miles north-east of York.

The river Rush empties into the lake eighteen miles below York, and is navigable for boats twenty miles up.

The river Credit, one of the best rivers in Canada for salmon, is tolerably large, and empties into lake Ontario about fifteen miles above York.

The Sixteen mile creek empties into the lake a few miles further up, is large, and also well stocked with fish; the Twelve mile creek empties itself about five miles further up, and is a beautiful stream.

The Chippewa river runs into the Niagara river, three miles above the falls; what is called the Twenty mile creek, has its rise near the head of the Chippewa, and empties into lake Ontario sixteen miles west of Niagara.

The Fifteen, Sixteen, Seventeen, Thirty and Forty miles creeks all run into lake Ontario, rushing over the slope affording fine falls.

The Grand river is a considerably large stream, of exceedingly clear water, rising from lake St. Clie, and is navigable for vessels of a considerable size, for fifty miles from its mouth; it empties into lake Erie, sixty miles from the east end, and contains many fine fish.

There is also the Thames, a large and beautiful river, rising near the head of Grand river, and emptying about thirty miles above Sandwich into the head of lake Erie; there are, also, a number of fine streams running into lake Erie, such as Big creek, passing through Houghton and Middleton township, and Kettle and Otter creeks, in Middlesex county.

There are not many villages in the province of Upper Canada, of much note, the inhabitants finding their greatest advantage in agriculture, the land being very cheap and fertile. The following are a few of the most notable.

CORNWALL is situate about one hundred and thirty miles down the river St. Lawrence, and is handsome, but small.

PRESCOTT is situate seventy miles below, standing opposite to Ogdensburg, on the United States side; it is an inconsiderable place, and there is a fort and a garrison.

BROCKVILLE lies twelve miles higher up the the river, and is handsomely situated, containing about eighty houses.

KINGSTON stands a few miles below the head of the St. Lawrence, opposite to Wolf island, which is the means of forming a safe and commodious harbour. It contains about one hundred aud fifty houses, a court house, jail, and two houses for public worship. The fort in this place is temporary, and the cannon small. It is a place of considerable commerical business, and is rapidly increasing.

YORK is situate one hundred and seventy miles south-west of Kingston, on the northern shore of lake Ontario, and is somewhat larger. It is laid out very much in the manner of Philadelphia, the streets intersecting each other at right angles. It is the seat of government, and contains some fine buildings, among which are a court-house, council house, and king's store house. The harbour is safe and beautiful, affording every convenience to shipping, and is so situate, that while the water of the main lake is tossed like the waves of the sea, it remains perfectly smooth and calm.

NIAGARA is situate on the south side of the lake, almost opposite York, at the point of land formed by the junction of the outlets of lakes Erie and Ontario. It is a beautiful, prospective situation, being surrounded on two sides by water, the lake on the north, and the Niagara river on the east, which affords a fine harbour. There are many squares of ground in this village adorned with almost every species of rare fruit. It is a place of considerable business, and is inhabited by an industrious and intelligent people.

QUEENSTOWN lies seven miles further up the Niagara. It is a small but handsome village; the most of the honses are built of stone or brick, and are large and well finished. Here also is done considerable business, and there are some very wealthy residents.

CHIPPEWA is situate ten miles above Queenston, and two above the falls of Niagara, at the mouth of the Chippewa Creek. It contains some handsome buildings.

FORT ERIE. 'There is a small village here of considerable beauty.—The inhabitants carry on a considerable traffic from the lake.

TURKEY POINT is situated about sixty miles south-west of Fort Erie, on the Lake shore, in the district of London, a little north of Long Point. It stands in a beautiful situation, is surrounded by a fertile country, and has a handsome court-house and jail.

PORT TALBERT lies sixty-four miles farther to the south-west, on the lake shore; a town was laid out here in 1807, and bids fair for a considerable place. It has a fine harbor for shipping.

MALDEN, this fort and village is situate on the south-west end of lake Erie, fourteen miles south of Detroit. It is a pleasant, though not a large place, and the fort is a strong one. On the twenty-seventh of September, 1813, this fort was burned by the British, on the approach of Harrison, previous to the battle of Moravian Town.

SANDWICH is situate still farther up the river, opposite Detroit, and is a handsome village of considerable age, inhabited chiefly by French.

There are several other villages in the province not immediately situate upon the water, which are of considerable size and beauty, but those already named are the principal.

The province of Upper Canada is divided into eight districts, twenty-four counties, and one hundred and fifty-six townships, generally about twelve miles square, these are subdivided into townships, and each township into fourteen concessions, the whole of which make two thousand one hundred and eighty-four. These concessions are divided into twenty-four lots of two hundred acres each, the whole of which amounts to thirty-two thousand, four hundred and sixteen, which number multiplied by two hundred, will produce ten million, four hundred and eighty-three thousand, two hundred, the number of acres surveyed in the province, besides considerable called broken fronts, not yet surveyed, but granted to those who owned land in the rear thereof. Between every concession there are four roods left for the public roads, and also between every fourth lot, which is one quarter of a mile wide.

Amongst the curiosities of the province of Upper Canada, the Falls of Niagara stand conspicuous; a description of them, therefore, cannot fail to be highly interesting:—

"In order to have a proper view of the Falls and the adjacent parts, I will suppose a person to be sailing in a little boat, out of Lake Ontario, up the Niagara river, or outlet of Lake Erie. Soon after you leave the Lake, you pass the village of Niagara on the right hand, and Niagara old fort on the United States side. A little farther up you pass Fort George on the right—here the water is deep and smooth. You still sail on a due south course, the water being smooth and the banks about sixteen feet high, and in most places perpendicular for seven miles. Here you come to Queenston on the right hand, and Lewiston on the left. This place is called the "landing," for here all the lading of vessels destined for the country, each side of Lake Erie and the Michigan territory are taken out, and conveyed up the mountain or slope, nine miles, to the still water, two miles above the Fall. The ascent of this slope, though three hundred feet high, is very easy. The river here is half a mile wide, and a little above there is a whirl of considerable depth, though not dangerous. After you pass this place three hundred yards, you enter the dismal chime, and instead of the lively prospect of the sailing of ships, with flying colors, fruitful fields, and pleasant landscapes, you are all at once buried in a grave, of at least three hundred feet deep. Although it is open in the top, should you look up, the sight is truly gloomy—the banks are perpendicular, and in some places more than perpendicular, abounding with craggy rocks, hanging over your head in a frightful manner; near the surface, there are to be seen flat rocks, projecting towards each other in a horizontal position. You still row on a south direction, with little variation; the water is considerably rapid, and the banks have nearly the same appearance, until within about a mile of the cataract, where the banks are not quite so high; but still all is gloomy, as you are buried from the sight of the land of the living, and must be filled with haunted thoughts of five hundred murdered dead,* that in one fatal hour plunged into the mighty grave, in which you now are.

As you proceed, the water becomes very rapid, and at length the mighty Falls appear in full, tremendous view, and fill the ear with dismal roar. It is eight miles from Queenston. When you arrive within three hundred yards of the cataract, you must stop. Here the bed of the river widens, and is not sunk more than half of the distance below the surface, as it was at your first entrance of the chime. A view of the horizon is more extensive. In sitting in your little bark the above distance, with your face to the south, before you flows the main body of water, and plunges over with a tremendous dash. About sixty yards of the middle of this cataract is much deeper than the rest, in consequence of a chime sunk in the rock. The water has a blueish green appearance. On your left hand comes the other part of the river, not so large by a sixth part, and falls over also.

This river is divided into two separate pitches, each four hundred yards in width. This division is made by a small island, crowding up to the verge of the rock, near the middle. It extends half a mile up the stream, and terminates in a point, where the water divides to the right and left.

*Down this dreadful chime, a number of American soldiers were driven headlong by the Indians, after they had surrendered themselves prisoners of war to the British, on the thirteenth of October, eighteen hundred and twelve.

The form of the cataract bends inward, or is nearly a semicircle. By the striking force of the falling water upon that below, wind is pressed under, which rises below in a foaming manner, though not to any heighth or violence.

The lime stone rock on the United States side over which the water flows, shelves considerably, and leaves a large cavity between the base and falling column of water, and, were it not for the depression of air, a person might walk some distance in it without being wet.

The mighty dash of so great a body of water on the bed below, raises a fog or small rain, which mounts up two thousand feet, in which, when the sun shines, may be seen a variety of beautiful rain-bows. This fog spreads to a considerable distance, and proves a fecundating moisture for the circumjacent woods and fields, the superior freshness and luxury of which are strikingly perceptible. This fog can be seen in clear weather for forty miles, particularly by persons on the lakes, and often serves as a guide for sailing.

In the winter this rain falling upon the neighboring trees, congeals in a thousand shapes, forming a romantic and pleasing appearance.

About half a mile above the falls, what are called the rapids begin, and descend fifty feet to the cataract. The draft of this rapid is so great, that it often reaches ducks and geese, when they appear to be half a mile out of danger, and when once under the influence of the impetuous current, they cannot get on the wing again. Indians, with their canoes, have been known to be irresistably carried down the rapid, and have disappeared forever.

Above the rapid, the river spreads to nearly three miles wide, and is shallow, with several small islands.

The river now has a south-east course to Grand Island, nine miles wide, and then south to lake Erie, where it is only a mile wide. This is twenty miles from the falls by water, from this place you may sail more than a thousand miles, if you wish, without encountering any more falls.

If my reader pleases, I will invite him back again to view and contemplate a little more, this awful scene. On both sides of the rapids, above the falls, the banks of the river are quite low; and there are many convenient situations for water works. Several are now erected, yet there is room for more. With a small expense a large quantity of water can be brought in use to do great execution.

The perpendicular pitch of this vast body of water is one hundred and forty-four feet, add to this fifty feet which the water descends, above the falls, and seventy feet below, and we find that the river descends in eight miles and a half, two hundred and sixty-four feet. Some who have never seen this river suppose it to be much less than it is, and others suppose it to be larger; indeed it is hard for any one to judge with propriety, that has seen it, as there are but eight miles in the whole length of the river, between the two lakes, where any current can be seen, and that is very rapid.

For the contemplation of the curious, who may, perhaps, never see these falls, I have made the following calculation, from which they may form some tolerable correct idea of the quantity of water that falls over this cataract.

Say that each of the spaces, over which the water pitches, is four hundred yards wide, or twelve hundred feet; the most shallow one of these, or that on the United States' side, is three feet deep on the verge of the rock, over which it falls. Now if we multiply its depth three feet, into its width, twelve hundred feet, we have thirty-six hundred cubic, or solid feet of water, on the verge of the precipice. As there are sixty-two pounds avoirdupoise, in a cubic or solid foot of water, and a little more, which we leave out to avoid fractions, so if we multiply sixty-two, the pounds in a square foot of water, by thirty-six hundred, the number of feet of water on the verge, we have, two hundred and twenty-three thousand, two pounds of water, on the verge of the precipice. But when we consider the laws of gravity respecting spouting fluids and falling bodies, we shall find the water of this cataract, receives a vast additional weight by the time it comes to the lowest point of fall. In order therefore to find this additional weight, we must note the following things:—"Heavy bodies near the surface of the earth, fall one foot the first quarter of a second, three feet the second, five the third, and seven feet in the fourth quarter; that is sixteen feet in the first second. Let go three bullets together, stop the first at one second, and it will have fallen sixteen feet; stop the next at the end of the second second, it will have fallen, four times sixteen, or sixty-four feet; stop the last at the end of the third second and the distance it will have fallen will be nine times sixteen or one hundred and forty-four feet, and so on. Now the momentum or force with which a falling body strikes, is equal to its weight multiplied by its velocity," and in order to find which we must multiply the perpendicular space fallen through by sixty-four, and the square root of the product is the velocity required.— *See Pike's Arithmetic, pages 362 and 5.*

From calculation, we find that the water of the cataract is three seconds descending the one hundred and forty-four feet, and that the velocity acquired in that time and distance to be ninety-six, which, if we multiply into two hundred and twenty-three thousand, the number of pounds of water on the top of the rock, we find that twenty-one millions four hundred and twenty-seven thousand two hundred is the weight thereof, at the lowest point of fall—This is the weight of the water at the smallest part of the cataract, or that on the United States' side. The other part of the Falls, as has been noted, is at least six times as large; that is, six times the quantity of water flows over. Now if we multiply the above sum, 21,427,200 by six, we shall have the enormous sum of 128,563,200 lbs. of water, which falls on the bed of the river below."

About two miles above the Falls, there is a spring of water, whose vapour is highly inflammable, and is emitted, for a time, with a considerable degree of force. If gathered into a narrow compass, it will support combustion for twenty minutes, and is capable of communicating to water, placed in a confined vessel and held over it, the degrees of boiling temperature.

There is also, at some distance below the Falls, a large hole, called the Devil's Hole; it is three hundred yards in circumference, and three hundred feet deep, with trees and craggy rocks sticking to the inner surface. There is supposed to be a considerable depth of water at the bottom.

What is called the Mountain Lake, may also be termed one of the curiosities of this portion of country; it is situated in Prince Edward County, on the shore, about thirty miles from Kingston, on the top of a mountain of about two hundred feet in height—it is three miles round, and, what is a curious circumstance, is well stocked with fish, although being in no manner connected with the bay or lake, except by a small stream that flows from it into the bay, by a perpendicular descent.

There are also many other curiosities, which the limits of this work will not allow of being noticed. Among these may be counted the Whirlpool, about three miles below the Falls, and four above Queenston; as also the many falls in Twenty Mile Creek, which, like the Niagara, flows over the same mountain. One of these falls has a perpendicular descent of seventy-seven feet, and the water, after running for some time with great violence, falls over again, presenting to the admirer of nature a most imposing spectacle.

# DESCRIPTION

## OF

# LOWER CANADA.

This province lies on both sides of the river St. Lawrence, between forty-five and fifty-two degrees of north latitude, and sixty-one and eighty degrees west longitude, from Greenwich. It is bounded on the north by New-Britain, on the east by the gulf of the St. Lawrence, on the south east by New-Brunswick, the district of Maine, and New Hampshire: south by Vermont, and seventy-five miles of the state of New-York, viz: from lake Champlain to the St. Regis river, where it empties into the St. Lawrence; and on the west by Upper Canada.

Upon the north line it extends to a distance of six hundred and eighty-five miles; its extent on the south line is nearly nine hundred miles, and measures in the middle about four hundred and fifty miles, running narrower to each end, more especially to the north-eastern one. The dividing line between this and the upper province, takes its commencement from the north side of lake St. Francis; it then pursues nearly a north course, running nearly twenty miles to the Ottawas river, which comes from the north-west, and falls into the St. Lawrence at Montreal, it then ascends that river to longitude eighty west, thence it takes a due north course to Charlton Island, about the middle of the south end of James' Bay, where it intersects the north line in north latitude fifty-two, and west longitude eighty.

The climate of this province is any thing but pleasant, during the winter, which lasts six months, commencing in November and finishing in the latter end of April, there are continual falls of snow, which lie generally to the depth of from four to five feet. The mercury in the thermometer, in this province, has been known to freeze, and in summer time it sometimes rises to ninety-six degrees; when, however the winter breaks up, the growth of vegetation is really surprising. Yet notwithstanding the intense heat of summer, and the rigor of winter, the inhabitants enjoy excellent health, and are vigorous and robust, carrying a strength, quite unusual to more southern climates, even to a very advanced age.

The ice on the rivers and lakes of Lower Canada generally acquires a thickness of two feet, and is capable of sustaining almost any weight—that on the borders of the St. Lawrence sometimes exceeds six feet.

As regards variety of soil the province of Lower Canada can vie with almost any other; the traveller may be for many days delighted with the prospect of the most luxurious vegetation, and landscapes, improved by art and industry, and in a transition which he feels to be almost sudden, finds himself surrounded on all sides by barrenness and desolation, without one solitary object upon which the eye may rest with pleasure. On all the low banks of the St. Lawrence, the soil is good, as it is on the low grounds of other large rivers. Some of the vallies not situate on rivers afford excellent land; it is generally of a black mould, mixed with a small portion of sand. On the higher grounds the soil is of a more sandy nature and is mixed slightly with blue clay. On the high hills and mountains, it is clay and gravel—lime-stone is found in great plenty, in many places of this province, and answers an excellent purpose.

In the northern part of the province there are many very large and shallow ponds of water, abounding with animals of the fur kind, which in summer time become partly dried up, creating an unwholesome effluvia; these if they were drained would make excellent meadow land, and many of them might be thus converted into good land at a very trifling expense.

There are two sorts of pine in this province, the white and the red, which are excellent for the East Indies; four sorts of firs, two sorts of cedar and oak, the white and the red; the male and female maple; three sorts of ash trees, the free, the mongrel and the bastard; three sorts of walnut trees, the hard, the soft, and the smooth; vast numbers of beech trees and white wood, white and red elms and poplars. The Indians hollow the red elms into canoes, some of which, made out of one piece, will contain twenty persons; others are made of the bark, the different pieces of which they sew together, with the inner rind, and daub over the seams with pitch, or rather bituminous substance resembling pitch, to prevent their leaking. The ribs of these canoes are made of boughs of trees. In the hollow elms, the bears and wild cats take up their residence from November to April.

In every part of the province there are plenty of evergreens, such as hemlock, cedar, firs, holly and laurel, with others. Many of these evergreens are loaded with an abundance of moss, which has a romantic appearance, and affords fine shelter for wild beasts and fowl, in the winter season. Here may be found large spots of ground under natural roofs, covered with dry leaves, while the snow is five feet deep on the surrounding parts, a circumstance extremely beneficial to the Indians, and the animals of this cold region. To these places the Indians resort for hunting purposes, and here screened from the wind they lie down upon the dry leaves beside their fire and feel as comfortable as the rich farmer or merchant in his warm house. One who has never been at these places can form no correct idea of the great difference of the weather in these solitary retreats.

There is also a great variety of wild fruit, particularly the crab-apple, potatoe, onion and cranberry.

Near Quebec there has been found an excellent lead mine, and many valuable ones of iron, have also been discovered at different places. Some silver, it is said, has also been found in the mountains. There have also been found some coal mines, the coal from which burns well, and some of alum, copperas and clays, that paint quite well.

Fifty miles from Quebec on the banks of the "*Trois Rivieres,*" there is an excellent mine of iron ore, it lies horizontal, situate near the surface, and is composed of masses easily detached from each other, perforated, and the holes filled with ochre. It possesses softness and pliability, and for promoting its fusion a grey limestone, found in its vicinity is used. The hammered iron is soft and tenacious, and has the quality of not being subject to rust.

The lakes of Lower Canada are numerous, though not large; a considerable number of which have no names; the first, however, of any note, is that of Black river, from which the river has its source; it lies in north latitude fifty-one, and west longitude sixty-six, forty-eight, is of considerable depth, and about one hundred miles in circumference.

Middle Lake lies about one hundred miles to the west of the former, is small, and is the source of Bustard river, which empties into the St. Lawrence, and passes through several lakes; also, a vast number of lakes are to be found in every direction from the lake.

Lake St. John is situate about one hundred miles north of Quebec, and is about ninety miles in circumference. This lake is the source of the river Saquenay. Another considerable lake is also found, one hundred miles to the north-west, near the great chain of mountains; it is the source of Picksuagus river.

Abbitib Lake is situate in latitude forty-nine, and longitude seventy-nine, and is the source of a large river of the same name, which runs into the south end of James' Bay. It is one hundred and ninety miles in circumference, tolerably shallow, and abounds with small islands. In the vicinity of this lake are several more of less note.

Lake Mistissiney is situated north of Quebec about two hundred and fifty miles, and is about three hundred miles in circuit, though a number of points of land extend into it a good distance from every direction. It is the source of Rupert's River, which passes through some small lakes, on its way to James' Bay, a north-east course.

Lake St. Charles is situate north of Quebec, and receives and discharges the river St. Charles; it is about five miles long.

Lake Megantic, lies south of Quebec, about ninety miles, and is the source of the river Chaudiere.

Lake Calvier is small, and is situated a few miles above Quebec.

Lake St. Peter is formed by the expansion of the St. Laurence, to the breadth of twenty miles. It is one hundred and twelve miles from Quebec.

The lake of the Two Mountains, and the lake of St. Louis, are in the vicinity of Montreal; the latter is formed by the junction of the Ottawas, with the St. Laurence. The lake of the Two Mountains is an expansion of the Ottawas, ten miles above its mouth, and is twenty miles long, and three broad.

The rivers of Lower Canada are very numerous, and chiefly run into the St. Laurence; the most of them come from the north, and afford many romantic falls.

In sailing up the gulf of St. Lawrence, the first river of note which is seen, is the *Moisic river;* about forty miles further up, we come to *Machigabiou river:* and in forty more, we come to *Black river*, already noted; this river is three hundred miles long, and quite large, and falls into the St. Lawrence, some distance above the gulf.

The next in course is *Bustard river*, about ten miles further up. This is one of the longest rivers of Lower Canada. It falls into the St. Laurence in lat. 48.50, north, after running a course of at least four hundred miles.

*Betsaimites river*, appears next in sailing up the St. Laurence. It is large, of considerable length, and passes through several lakes.

*Portnus*, is a river of some length, coming from two small lakes. It empties into the St. Laurence, fifty miles above.

*Pepe Chaisinagau river*, succeeds in course, and falls into the St. Laurence, twenty miles above Portnus.

In sailing up the St. Laurence, several small streams are seen; at length we come to *St. James' river;* and a little distance above, we come to the river *Saguenay*, which rises out of lake St. John, already noted; which lake is the repository of four considerable rivers, with their numerous branches, viz: those of the *Picksuaganis, Chissouematon, Sable,* and *Periboaca*. In its course, the Saguenay receives the *Missiguinipi*, and several more of considerable size, after which, it falls into the St. Laurence, one hundred and fifty miles below Quebec, from nearly a west direction. This river is one hundred and fifty miles in length, from the lake; and sweeps along a prodigious quantity of water. It is interrupted in its course, by abrupt precipices, over which it dashes its foaming current; and being bounded by banks of great elevation, is remarkable for the depth and impetuosity of its flood, which is sensibly felt in the St. Laurence, whose water is obliged to yield to its impulse for a distance of several miles. Large vessels, apparently going their course, have thereby been carried side-long in a different direction.

This river, is generally, three miles wide, except at its mouth, where it is only one; at which place, five hundred fathoms of line have been let down, without finding any bottom. Two miles up, it is one hundred and thirty-eight fathoms, and at sixty miles, it is sixty fathoms deep.

Albany river succeeds next in course, which rises in a small lake, about sixty miles north from the St. Laurence, and flows through the fertile valley of Mal-bay. This river abounds with salmon and other excellent fish.

*Montmorenci* is the next considerable river, and falls into the St. Laurence, eight miles below Quebec, over a precipice of two hundred and forty-six feet.

*St. Charles*, falls into the same close by Quebec, and is of considerable size.

On the south side of the gulf and river St. Laurence, there are a number of streams, which fall into it, and take their rise in New Brunswick, New Hampshire and Vermont.

The largest is the *Chandiere* river, rising out of lake Megantic, and flowing a north course, one hundred and thirty miles, falls into the St. Laurence about eight miles above Quebec. Ships sail some distance up this river.

The river *St. Nicholas*, falls in on the same side of the St. Laurence, but a little higher up. *Jacques Cartier*, a river of considerable size, falls into the St. Laurence, about thirty miles above Quebec. The stream of this, like all the rivers in Lower Canada, is frequently broken into cascades, affording picturesque scenery.

The *St. Ann*, and *Dog rivers*, are streams of some note, and fall into the St. Laurence, from the north.

*Batiscan river*, also flows from the north, into the St. Laurence. *Three Rivers*, otherwise, called *St. Maurice*, falls into the St. Laurence, from the north, fifty miles above Quebec, by three mouths. It is three hundred miles long, and much navigated by the Indians, from the vicinity of Hudson bay. The tide of the St. Laurence flows no higher than the mouth of this river.

*St. Reges river*, rises in the state of New-York, and falls into the upper end of lake St. Francis, in lat. 45 degrees. This is the last river of Lower Canada, which runs into the St. Laurence, from the south.

*Ottawas river*, is one of the largest in Upper Canada, except the St. Laurence, into which it falls below, and above Montreal, as has been noted. It is at least, one thousand miles long; one of its branches, the *Petite Riviere*, rises out of lake Tomis-Cauting, and after meeting together four hundred miles from Montreal, receives a number of tributary streams on its way, and pitches over a number of precipices.

All the rivers as yet described, run into the St. Laurence from the south or north; there are several which run into James' bay, after running a western or north eastern course—viz.

*Slude river* and *Rupert's river*, which has a course of nearly two hundred miles; and Harraconaw river, which empties into the south end of James' bay, and is a beautiful river.

*The river St. Lawrence* is one of the greatest, and most beautiful rivers; from its mouth to Montreal, the head of ship navigation, it is five hundred and forty-five miles: for one thousand more it is passed by very large boats, from here, for two hundred and forty miles, through lake Ontario, the largest vessels in the world may sail.

The harbors in Lower Canada are numerous, chiefly situate in the St. Laurence; there are a few on lake Champlain, and two or three on the north-west coast of James' Bay.

Fish, of which there is a great variety, is very plenty.

There are but two cities in Lower Canada, Quebec and Montreal, (a description of these may be found in the memoirs.)

Considering the great extent of Lower Canada, its villages are few in number, and small in size, chiefly lying on the banks of the St. Laurence.

The first of any note above Quebec, for there are none below, is *Jeunne Lorette;* it lies nine miles north west of Quebec, and contains fifty log houses, inhabited by French and some Indians; there is a decent chapel in this village.

The village of *Trois Rivieres*, is situate on the north bank of the St. Laurence, extends three fourths of a mile long, and contains seventy houses and a church.

*Charlebourg* is situate eighty miles east of Lorette, and is something larger.

The village of *William Henry* or *Sorel* is agreeably situate at the confluence of the Sorel or Chambly river with the St. Laurence, and contains a Protestant and Roman Catholic house for divine worship.

Some distance above Sorel, is is situate *Vercheres;* it contains about forty houses.

*Sault Saint Louis*, is a small village of about one hundred and fifty houses, inhabited chiefly by the Iroquois or Mohawk Indians. It is about sixteen miles above Montreal, and was originally built for those Indians, who have long been converted to the christian religion. It is chiefly built of stone. The church and dwelling of the missionaries are protected by a stone wall, in which there are loop holes for musquetry.

*Point aux Trembles* village is fifty-one miles from Quebec, contains one hundred and twenty houses, a small convent of nuns, and a neat church.

The village of the *Cedars* is charmingly situated on the St. Laurence, not far above Montreal; it contains about fifty houses.

The *Canasadago* village of the Iroquois, a Mohawk, and Algonquin tribes of Indians, is situate on a delightful point of land on the hills, on the east side of the two mountains, in the Ottowas river. Near the extremity of the Point, their church is built, which divides the village into two parts, forming a regular angle along the water side. It contains about two hundred houses, and two thousand five hundred souls.

The province of Lower Canada is divided into three districts and twenty-one counties, viz: Gaspe, Cornwallis, Devon, Hertford, Dorchester, Buckinghamshire, Richlieu, Bedford, Surrey, Kent, Huntington, York, Montreal, Effingham, Leinster, Warwick, St. Maurice, Hampshire, Quebec, Northumberland and Orleans. These counties are subdivided into parishes.

The only natural curiosities worth naming in Lower Canada, are those cascades and water-falls with which the province abounds.

The Bird Isles, which are situate in the gulf of St. Laurence, consist of two rocks elevated above the water, upwards of one hundred feet, their flattened summits, whose circumference does not exceed three hundred yards, exhibit a resplendent whiteness, produced by the quantities of ordure with which they are covered, from immense flocks of birds, which, in summer, take possession of the apertures in their perpendicular cliffs, where they form their nests, and produce their young. When alarmed, they hover above the rocks, and overshadow their tops by their numbers. The abundance of their eggs affords to the inhabitants of the neighboring coast, a material supply of food.

Ninety miles up the Saguenay river, already noted, there is a fall of water, that deserves notice, chiefly on account of the immense sheet of water, which is perperpetually broken in its rugged course, and assumes a resplendent whiteness.

When viewed from below the scene is stupendous and terrific. The incessant and deafening roar of the waters and the violence with which they hasten to their descent, tend to produce on the mind of the spectator an impression awfully grand. The picturesque and rudely wild forms of the lofty banks, exhibit a gloomy contrast to the lively splendors of the cataract.

Three hundred and thirty miles from the mouth of the St. Laurence is situate Cape Tourment, whose perpendicular altitude is two thousand feet. It exhibits a grand and sublime view, especially to those sailing up the river.

The cataract of the river Montmorencie, which empties into the St. Laurence, eight miles below Quebec, may be reckoned among the natural curiosities of this country. The following description is in the words of Mr. Herriott:

"After exhibiting a grateful variety throughout its course, the Montmorenci is precipitated in an almost perpendicular direction, over a rock of the height of two hundred and forty-six feet; falling, when it touches the rock, in white clouds of rolling foam; and underneath, where it is propelled with uninterrupted gravitation, in numerous flakes, like wool or cotton, which are gradually protracted in their descent, until they are received in the boiling profound abyss below."

"Viewed from the summit of the cliff, from whence they are thrown, the waters, with every concommitant circumstance, produce an effect equally grand, and wonderfully sublime. The prodigious depth of their descent, the brightness and volubility of their course, the swiftness of their movement through the air, and the loud and hollow noise emitted from the basin, swelling with incessant agitation, from the weight of the dashing waters, forcibly combine to attract the attention, and to impress with sentiments of grandeur and elevation, the mind of the spectator. The clouds of vapor arising and assuming the prismatic colors, contribute to enliven the scene. They fly off from the fall, in the form of a revolving sphere, emitting with velocity pointed flakes of spray, which spread in receding, until intercepted by neighboring banks, or dissolved in the atmosphere."

" The breadth of the fall is one hundred feet; the basin is bounded by steep cliffs, composed of grey lime slate, lying in inclined strata, which on the east and west sides, are sub-divided into innumerable thin shivers, forming with the horizon an angle of forty-five degrees, and containing between them fibrous gypsum, and *pierre a calumet*, a soft stone of which the heads of pipes are sometimes formed, mouldering incessantly by exposure to the air, and the action of the weather; no surface for vegetation remains upon these substances."

Eight miles from Quebec, the river Chaudiere empties into the south side of St. Laurence; and four miles from its mouth, there is a beautiful cataract, which deserves attention.

The month of May, appears to be the most advantageous period, at which to contemplate this interesting scene, the approach to which ought first to be made, from the top of the banks; as in emerging from the woods, it conducts at once to the summit of the cataract, where the objects which instantaneously become developed to the eye, strike the mind with surprise, and produce a powerful impression.

"The water descends from a height of one hundred and twenty feet, and being separated by rocks, forms three separate cataracts; the largest of which, is on the western side, and they unite in the basin, beneath their broken and agitated waters. The form of the rock forces a part of the water, into an oblique direction, and advances them beyond the line of the precipice. The cavities worn in the rocks, produce a pleasing variety, and cause the descending waters to revolve with foaming fury, to whose whiteness the gloomy cliffs present a strong opposition of color. The vapor from each division of the falls, quickly mounting through the air, bestows an enlivening beauty on the landscape.

The wild diversity displayed by the banks of the stream, and the foliage of the overhanging woods, the brilliancy of colors richly contrasted, the rapidity of motion, the refulgent brightness of the cataracts, the deep and solemn sound, which they emit, and the various cascades further down the river, unite in rendering this such a pleasing exhibition of natural objects as few scenes can surpass."

" On descending the side of the river, the landscape becomes considerably altered, and the falls appear to great advantage. Masses of rocks and elevated points of land, covered with trees, together with the smaller cascades on the stream, present a rich assemblage, terminated by the falls. The scenery, in proceeding down the river, is rugged and wild.

" Viewed in the Winter season, the falls exhibit an appearance more curious than pleasing, being for the greatest part congealed, and the general form of the congealed masses, is that of a concretion of icicles, which resembles a cluster of pillars in Gothic architecture; and may not improperly be compared to the pipes of an organ. The spray becomes likewise consolidated into three masses, or secretions of a cone, externally convex, but concave toward the falls. The west side being usually the only place in which the waters flow; the aspect is infinitely inferior to that, displayed in Summer; and the sound emitted is comparatively faint. The surrounding objects, covered alike with snow, produce one uniform glare. The rocks and the bed of the river, disguised by unshapely white masses produce a reflection, which gives, even to the waters of the cataract, an apparent tinge of obscurity."

In the midst of the low ground, near cape Tourment, a narrow hill, about a mile in length, and flatted on its summit, rises to the height of one hundred feet. Upon the top is erected a large dwelling house, and a chapel; and thither the ecclesiastics of the seminary of Quebec, to whom the land belongs, retire in the Summer.

There are many other curiosities in this province, which cannot here be described; those most remarkable, however, have already been noted.

Almost all the inhabitants of Lower Canada, that have come to the years of maturity, are professors of religion—the great majority are of the Roman Catholic persuasion, for whose worship, some years back, there were one hundred and thirty churches, seven convents, one hundred and ninety secular and regular priests, and one bishop. There were also sixteen clergymen of the church of England, and one bishop, besides some Presbyterians, Baptists, Methodists and Quakers; all of whom enjoy freedom of conscience, unmolested.

The Roman Catholic clergy of the province are distinguished for their devotion, benevolence, and inoffensive conduct and humanity. They are regular and rigid in their religious ceremonies.

In the year 1497, Lower Canada was discovered by John Cabot, a Venetian in the service of the English.

In 1534, Jacques Cartier, a Frenchman, under commission of Frances I, explored the gulf of St. Lawrence, and the next year ascended the river, and wintered at St. Croix, where he erected a wooden cross.

In 1603, a patent for an exclusive trade was granted to Sieur de Monts, who employed Champlain to make further discoveries in Canada.

In 1608, Champlain sailed up the St. Laurence, as far as a strait, called by the Indians Quebec, which is the mouth of Sorrell river, where, on the third of July, he began to build, and here passed the following Winter. At this time, the settlement of Canada commenced.

In 1628, a company of rich merchants, one hundred and seven in number, was established by patent, for an exclusive trade.

This company acquired a right of soil, in 1642; but their charter was revoked in 1663.

In 1629, Quebec was taken by the English, under Sir David Keith; and surrendered to the French by the treaty of St. Germain.

In 1690, Sir Wm. Phipps, with an armament from Boston, made an unsuccessful attack upon Quebec.

On September 13, 1759, an English army under Gen. Wolfe, made a successful attack upon Quebec, which surrendered on the 18th.

In 1760, the whole province of Canada surrendered to Gen. Amherst, and was confirmed to Great-Britain by the treaty of 1763, under whose dominions it has since continued.

www.ingramcontent.com/pod-product-compliance
Lightning Source LLC
Chambersburg PA
CBHW020150170426
43199CB00010B/970